Women in Housing:

Access and Influence

By

MARION BRION AND ANTHEA TINKER

Published in 1980 by
The Housing Centre Trust
62 Chandos Place
London W.C.2

I.S.B.N. 0 950 2005 73

Printed in Great Britain by
Heffers Printers Ltd
Cambridge

DEDICATION

For

Eric and Stanley,
Jonathan, Andrew and Rachel,
Elizabeth and Julia

ACKNOWLEDGEMENTS

This book is based on work done during a period when we were both on the staff of The City University. The research was carried out independently and not as part of a sponsored research project. A small amount of the data used is taken from research work funded by the Department of the Environment and we acknowledge the permission of the Comptroller of Her Majesty's Stationery Office to quote from this and other official studies. We alone, however, are responsible for any errors there may be in this book and the conclusions. The views expressed must not be taken to represent those of the Department of the Environment, nor of the Housing Centre Trust which has agreed to act as publisher.

Our thanks go to our colleagues at The City University, especially the staff of the Library and to John Mason who had a shared interest in the historical work. We would like to thank the people who commented on the draft including Mrs Margaret Baker, Miss C. Christie, Miss Marjorie Cleaver, Mr Richard Edmonds, Mr Nicholas Giles, Dr Charles Legg, Professor Henry Maddick and Mrs Mary E. H. Smith. We also wish to express our gratitide to the authors and publishers of the passages we have quoted, and to the Institute of Housing for allowing us to use both their records and those of the Society of Housing Managers. We would particularly like to thank those members of the Society and the Institute who agreed to be interviewed. We are also very grateful to Mrs Carole Austin, Miss Helen Shepherd and Mrs Jenny Wren for typing the script.

Finally we would like to pay tribute to all the members of our families who have lived with Women in Housing for so long and have helped us in so many ways.

Contents

Page

ACKNOWLEDGEMENTS iv

ABBREVIATIONS USED x

1. INTRODUCTION 1
   Background 1
   The aims and outline of this study 1
   Sources of the data 3
   Limitations 3

PART ONE – ACCESS TO HOUSING

2. THE EFFECT OF MARRIAGE AND FAMILY STATUS . . . 4
   Introduction 4
   Law and women's rights in housing 6
   The effect of women's role on the design of housing 7
   Single women 9
      General
      Owner occupation
      Renting
      The special position of single women with elderly dependants
   Married Women 11
      General
      Married women in tied accommodation
   Women whose marriages break down 13
      General
      Owner occupation
      Renting
   Cohabitees 16
   Widows 17
   Conclusions 17
   References 17

3. DISADVANTAGED GROUPS 20
   Introduction 20
   The elderly 21
   The physically disabled 23
   The mentally disordered 24
   Single parents 25
   Battered women 27
   Homeless women 29
   Lower income households 30
   Others 31
   Conclusions 31
   References 32

4. HOW CHANGE HAS BEEN ACHIEVED AND WHAT
   REMAINS TO BE DONE   34
   Introduction   34
   The reasons for change   34
       Research, individuals, pressure groups and the media
       Women's greater financial independence, the women's move-
           ment and the Equal Opportunities Commission
   What is needed – introduction   36
   What is needed – easier access, greater rights and better condi-
       tions in each tenure   36
   What is needed – changes in provision and practice   40
       More of existing forms of provision
       Special types of accommodation
       Easier exchanges and transfers
       More advice for women
       Closer links between departments and agencies
   New approaches   44
       Positive discrimination?
       New types of tenure and provision?
       Changes in the law
   Conclusions   45
   References   46

PART TWO – WOMEN IN THE HOUSING SERVICE

5. THE GENERAL PICTURE   48
   Introduction   48
   Women employed in housing organisations   48
       Central government
       Local government and housing associations
   Differences in the kind of work done by men and women   50
       Chief officers
       Section heads
       Basic level jobs
       Summing up
   Factors which might affect achievement   54
       Interest in housing as a career
       Educational qualifications
       Professional qualifications
   Conclusions   57
   References   58

Page

6. LOOKING BACK – OCTAVIA HILL AND THE BEGIN-
   NING OF HOUSING WORK FOR WOMEN   59
   Early influences   59
   Housing conditions   59
   The early work   60
   Growth in the scope of the work   61
   What was the Octavia Hill system?   62
   Assessments of Octavia Hill's work   64
   Other influential women   66
   References   67

7. THE RISE OF A WOMEN'S PROFESSIONAL HOUSING
   SOCIETY, 1912–1938   69
   The beginning of an association of women housing managers . . .   69
   Women get a foothold in local government   70
   The women's professional association 1933–38   72
   The employment of women
   Training
   General housing activities
   The Institute of Housing   74
   The two rival organisations: Institute and Society in 1938   75
   Membership
   Housing management practice
   References   77

8. THE WAR YEARS TO THE MID SIXTIES   78
   The war years   78
   The Institute   79
   The Society   80
   The admission of men
   Principles of housing management
   The move towards amalgamation   82
   The reasons behind the move towards unification
   Progress towards unification   86
   References   87

Page

9. WOMEN IN THE HOUSING SERVICE 1965–1977   88
    Introduction   88
    Committee members' views on changes in the Institute after
        unification   88
        The status of the professional body
        Social aspects
        Opportunities for women
    Membership of the council of the institute 1965–77   90
    Reasons for the lack of women council members   90
        The process of election
        Differing attitudes to service on the governing body
        Lack of participation generally
        An overview
    Changes in the distribution of qualified staff 1965–77   95
        Housing departments
        Housing associations
        'Other employers'
    The output of qualified staff   97
    Reasons for the changes in the position of women members . . .   99
        Change in the careers of women qualifying
        Housing work and the woman's role
        Growth in the size of housing organisations
        Housing management policy
        Discrimination?
    Conclusions   108
    References   109

PART THREE: WOMEN AND HOUSING POLICY

10. COUNCILLORS, MEMBERS OF PARLIAMENT AND
        PRESSURE GROUPS   111
    Local Government   111
        Participation of women as elected representatives
        Who are the leaders in local government?
        Women as chairmen of major committees
        Why are women not more influential in local government?
    Central government   116
        Ministers and Members of Parliament
        Members of advisory committees
    Pressure groups   122
    Conclusions   124
    References   124

Page

11. CONCLUSIONS 126
Summary of findings 126
The underlying causes 127
  Women live longer than men
  The average woman is smaller and less muscular than the
    average man
  Women and not men bear children
  The effect of stereotyped sex roles
  Different associative styles
Some reasons for the gains and losses 131
The way forward 136
  Attitudes
  Sharing the caring
  Sharing the work
  Affirmative action
  Changes in housing organisations
  Advice and support for women
  Better access to housing and more understanding of how
    housing problems affect women
Conclusions 144
References 144

APPENDIX: SOURCES OF THE DATA 146
Access to housing 146
Women in the housing service 146
  Statistics on women members of the Institute of Housing
  The interviews
  Records of the Society and the Institute
  The Education and Training for Housing Work Project
Councillors, M.P.s and pressure groups 148

SELECT BIBLIOGRAPHY 149

ABBREVIATIONS USED

A.P.	Administrative and professional grades in local government.
C.H.A.R.	The Campaign for the Homeless and Rootless.
C.H.A.C.	Central Housing Advisory Committee
C.S.O.	Central Statistical Office.
C.P.A.G.	Child Poverty Action Group.
D.E.P.	Department of Employment.
D.O.E.	Department of the Environment.
D.H.S.S.	Department of Health and Social Security.
E.O.C.	Equal Opportunities Commission.
F.E.S.	*Family Expenditure Survey.*
G.H.S.	*General Household Survey.*
H.O.H.	Head of Household.
H.M.S.O.	Her Majesty's Stationery Office.
I.O.H.	Institute of Housing.
M.P.	Member of Parliament.
M.H.L.G.	Ministry of Housing and Local Government.
M.O.H.	Ministry of Health.
N.A.L.G.O.	National and Local Government Officers Organisation.
N.C.S.W.D.	National Council for the Single Woman and her Dependants.
N.D.H.S.	*National Dwelling and Housing Survey.*
N.F.H.A.	National Federation of Housing Associations.
N.W.A.F.	National Women's Aid Federation.
O.P.C.S.	Office of Population, Censuses and Surveys.
P.O.	Principal Officer grade in local government.
P.R.O.	Public Record Office.
S.O.	Senior Officer grade in local government.
S.H.A.C.	Shelter Housing Aid Centre.
The Society	in 1916 the Association of Women Housing Workers was formed and in 1917 the name was changed to Association of Women House Property Managers. In 1932 this association and two other groups of women managers amalgamated to become the Society of Women Housing Estate Managers (S.W.H.E.M.). Succesive names were: 1937 Society of Women Housing Managers (Incorporated) (S.W.H.M.) and 1948 Society of Housing Managers (Incorporated) (S.H.M.). The latter was dissolved in 1965 and the Institute of Housing Managers formed by unification with the Institute of Housing.
S.B.C.	Supplementary Benefits Commission.
W.O.	Welsh Office.

CHAPTER 1

Introduction

Background

'A woman's place is in the home' sums up many traditional views about women. Women's magazines and radio and television programmes are full of features about 'home making', but they often start from the point where the home is already provided. It is assumed that women are just interested in what goes on in the home while men naturally hold the positions of authority as managers of building societies, as architects and as officers or elected representatives in public authorities.

It seems strange that as interest grows in the changing role of women so little attention has been focused on the wider aspects of the home. Yet housing is one of the most fundamental of human needs and the form it takes in any country at any period of history has depended on that society's social, economic and legal system. So it reflects clearly, among other things, the view of society at that time about the role of women. In this country even a superficial look at those involved in the processes of planning, designing and generally making decisions about housing shows that there are very few women among them, which is in sharp contrast to the very close interest that many women take in their homes.

This contrast struck the authors particularly forcibly. Both had for some years been concerned with housing and its administration and were working on separate research projects. One was concerned with housing the elderly, a group in which women predominate. The other was concerned with training for the housing service, where few women are to be found in positions of responsibility. These two projects indicated the contrast between the importance of women as 'consumers' in housing and their small role in the providing organisations. It seemed important to compare the level of their involvement as 'consumers' and as 'providers' and to try to identify the reasons for any differences.

The aims and outline of this study

The aim of this study is to consider the position of women both in relation to their opportunity of access to housing and also in relation to the authorities which provide or take decisions about this service. Are women now better able to gain and keep the housing which they need or want? Where are they disadvantaged and how has the position changed? What role do women play in the organisations which provide housing? Is their influence increasing or diminishing?

The first part of the book is concerned with women's access to housing. The idea of the dependency of women on a male relative has been very influential in determining the ability of women to obtain control over their housing. Chapter 2, therefore, considers the effect of law and marital status on women's access to housing. It is here that some of the major gains have been made. Chapter 3 discusses the difficulties of some of those groups of women generally recognised as disadvantaged. Chapter 4 examines the way in which improvements in women's access to housing have been gained and outlines some further steps that are needed.

In contrast to the improvements in access it appeared that women had made little headway in the housing service and that, possibly, their influence had diminished. Also, in contrast to the information about access, there was little published material on women in the housing service. It was decided, therefore, to study in greater detail women working in this field and to undertake some research from original sources.

So the second part of the book deals with women who are employed in housing organisations. After discussing what is known about the overall situation in Chapter 5, the employment of trained women in housing management is considered. Chapters 6, 7 and 8 trace the history of the women's professional organisation concerned with housing (the Society) and its unification with the Institute of Housing. Chapter 9 brings us back to the present day and considers the complex factors which affect women's participation in the Institute of Housing and in employment. Evidence from the historical study indicates that questions about the distribution of qualified women within housing organisations cannot be answered in any simplistic terms but that issues of power and prejudice are involved.

Then in Chapter 10 the position of women as policy makers in central and local government is examined. Here the position is less clear cut. While not making substantial inroads into posts of responsibility women are at least in a better position than in some other services. It was only possible to take a brief look at some of the other bodies involved in the formation of housing policy, such as pressure groups. It is interesting to note that the pattern of very few women in positions of influence is similar even in the voluntary bodies concerned with housing. The modest influence of women employed in the housing organisations is not in any way compensated for by a stronger presence on central or local bodies.

Finally, these various threads are drawn together, by looking at the underlying reasons why women have been disadvantaged and, in particular, considering why improvement in access to housing has not been paralleled by improvement in the other areas considered. We discuss what needs to be done so that the importance of housing to women can be reflected by their participation in decision making.

In this book we are concerned primarily with housing in Britain though much is common to Western society generally.

Sources of the data

This study uses completely new data as well as drawing together some existing sources of material. Most of the research was done in 1977–78 but some material has subsequently been updated.

The information on women's access to housing has been culled from a wide variety of sources. This includes official government publications and research published by both official and non-official bodies.

There were four major sources of data for the study of women in the housing service. The first was an analysis of statistics on women members of the Institute of Housing (I.O.H.) The second was interviews with all the members of the committee which dealt with the unification of the Society of Housing Managers and the Institute of Housing, together with certain key informants. Thirdly the records of the Society and Institute were studied. Fourthly information was obtained from the Department of the Environment (D.O.E.) funded study *The Education and Training for Housing Work Project* which took place at The City University from 1975–77.

The data on the influence of women as policy makers in housing is drawn mainly from official directories and reports such as *Hansard*. *The Municipal Year Books* for 1977 and 1978 gave information for the first time about membership of the major local authority committees. This has been analysed in detail on a sex basis. Material used by the Maud Committee (1967) in *Management of Local Government* and by the Robinson Committee (1977) in *Remuneration of Councillors* has also been included. An analysis was also carried out of the membership of the Central Housing Advisory Committee (C.H.A.C.) 1935–75, the Housing Services Advisory Group, various ad hoc committees concerned with housing 1965–75, committees connected with the New Towns and with some major pressure groups. Further details, and notes on the limitations of some of the data, are given in the Appendix.

Limitations

We are very much aware of the limitations of our work. For example we have not been able to look at the employment of women in the non public bodies influential in housing, such as building societies, development companies and building firms. Nor did we research the membership of committees of management of housing associations. We have only been able to include overall statistics about some of the allied professions, such as architecture and surveying. We look on what we have done as only a modest beginning from which others can pursue further research in specific areas. We hope that what we have written will be used to help women and men to understand how traditional sex roles have influenced the position of women in regard to housing and what could be done about this in the future.

CHAPTER 2

The Effect of Marriage and Family Status

Introduction

Housing is intimately related to the control of land and to the norms of society. Women have been particularly affected by two of these norms. The first, stretching far back in English law, is that a woman only exists as a dependent of a man. The second, which emerged somewhat later, is the particular importance of the nuclear family.

Taking first the position of a woman as a dependent, it is clear that at least from the middle ages women were generally perceived in this way. In a fascinating account of women in medieval society McNamara and Wemple describe the waxing and waning of women's influence and, in particular, their varied powers with regard to property.[1] A female has been regarded as dependent first on her parents and then on her husband. Women themselves, and their fortunes, could be regarded as 'property' to be disposed of by men. The only women to hold land (and therefore housing) in their own right were likely to be single women, who inherited it, or widows. Both were normally expected to seek male advice and protection as soon as possible. Some women did obtain positions of power but this was regarded as exceptional.

The idea of the woman as the dependent of man is so powerful and pervasive that it tends to pass unnoticed. Consider, for example, the concept 'Head of Household' (H.O.H.) used for much household data. In official surveys such as the *General Household Survey* (G.H.S.), the *Family Expenditure Survey* (F.E.S.) and, more recently, the *National Dwelling and Housing Survey* (N.D.H.S.) the head of household is assumed to be the man. This is made clear in the Government Social Survey's *A Handbook for Interviewers* where it is stated: "So long as the husband is resident he takes precedence over the wife in being H.O.H. This means if you have a married couple living together, even if the wife owns the property or has her name on the rent book, you count her husband as the H.O.H."[2] It is later made explicit that if two persons of different sex have an equal claim to be H.O.H. then it is the male who is to be designated. The patriarchal origins of this are now recognised and some demands for change are being made. However, having started surveys on this basis, it is argued that to change the definition would mean losing comparability with previous data. It is worth noting, however, that in the census the head of household is taken to be the person whose name appears first on the form. A household can, therefore, decide who the head will be.

With regard to the importance of the nuclear family, up to the time of the Reformation, and for some time afterwards, the ideal of society was an ordered patriarchal state in which each person had an accepted place. An extensive neighbourhood and kinship system played an important supportive role. Some writers have tended to idealise this kind of society, but in reality life was frequently disturbed by war and civil unrest and society always had its outcasts and its poor. The growth of capitalism and the coming of the industrial revolution disturbed this order and the extensive ties which supported it. Recent centuries have seen increasing stress put on the ideal of the nuclear family consisting of husband, wife and children.

Engels and later writers have firmly linked the enhanced role of the nuclear family with the needs of capitalism. They claim that the dual process under capitalism of women being confined to the home as housewives and of men losing control over their work and [their] pleasure in it, have given new importance to family life and put personal relationships under severe strain.[3] One does not have to agree with this argument to accept that the structure of the nuclear family has had great pressures exerted upon it and that marriages have increasingly been breaking down. Nor does the nuclear family correspond to the reality of the households in which many people live. It is true that most women do marry but the position is quite a complex one. Approximately 95 per cent of women marry at some time or other in their lives, about 30 per cent before they are 20 years old.[4] However, at any one time substantial numbers of them are single, widowed or divorced, and only two-thirds over the age of 15 will be married. The status of the remaining one-third varies according to age. In 1976 of those aged 15–44 most were single, but of those over 45 years of age the majority were widowed or divorced.[5]

The increased tendency for marriages to break down has already been noted. The divorce rate per thousand married population in 1951 was 2.6 and in 1977 10.4.[6] The total number of divorces made absolute in 1977 in the United Kingdom was 138,000.[7] In the *Family Formation* survey it was found that about one-tenth of the women who had contracted their first marriage between 1966 and 1970 had separated within five years.[8] Of the women who had married between 1961 and 1965 and later separated, just over half had formed new unions within six years – two-thirds of these were legal marriages and one-third cohabiting unions. The same survey noted that "Cohabitation is a much more common way of beginning a second union in the first two years after separation – partly because of the delay in obtaining a divorce."[9]

As we shall see later, the formation and breakdown of marriage and cohabiting unions, with or without children, are important factors in women's need for housing and for easy access to it. This is particularly important because of the widely held assumption that where a man is present the woman must be dependent on him.

Another powerful influence which should not be ignored is that of social class. It affects the kind of housing women expect to get, and even more markedly, what they actually achieve. This is brought out clearly in the *Family Formation* survey where it is suggested that, while young single women of all social classes have fairly similar housing expectations before marriage, there is a wide difference in what they actually achieve. In social class I, 63 per cent expected to buy a home of their own, 26 per cent to rent and none envisaged being without a home of their own (the rest did not know). In social class V, 55 per cent expected to buy, 36 per cent to rent and 9 per cent anticipated not having a home of their own. Although the groups are not strictly comparable what married women achieved showed wide gaps between expectations and achievements. At marriage only 13 per cent of social class I were without their own home compared with 54 per cent of social class V.[10]

Another interesting point about social class is that little comment seems to have been aroused by the statement in the survey *Family Formation* that "Single women's social class was assigned from their father's occupations whereas that of married women was based on their husband's occupation at first marriage."[11]

Because the twin concepts of the dependent status of women and the idealised nuclear family are so significant we need to consider briefly how these concepts have affected women's position in regard to the legal ownership of property and their influence on the design of housing.

Law and women's rights in housing

The view expressed in law has been that a woman was a dependent of a man. Women were expected to marry and the attitude to a married woman was based on the assumption that she was dependent on her husband and that her main role was to care for him and their children. It was not until the *Married Women's Property Act 1882* that a wife was legally able to hold property in her own right. Before this any property could only be held for her by a trustee and this was often her husband. A married woman could not even carry out a legal action in her own right. This position of almost complete dependency was challenged by the women's suffrage and women's rights movements, and a series of Acts over a long period of time have given women more rights to property. Key legislation includes:

1882 *Married Women's Property Act*
1925 *Law of Property Act*
1964 *Married Women's Property Act*
1967 *Matrimonial Homes Act*
1973 *Matrimonial Causes Act*
1975 *Sex Discrimination Act*
1976 *Domestic Violence and Matrimonial Proceedings Act*
1977 *The Housing (Homeless Persons) Act*
1978 *Domestic Proceedings and Magistrates Court Act*

These Acts are referred to in later sections of this book but one general piece of legislation must be considered here. Under the *Sex Discrimination Act 1975* a person is held to discriminate against a woman if, "on the grounds of her sex, he treats her less favourably than he treats or would treat a man, or he applies to her a requirement or condition which he applies or would apply equally to a man but which is such that the proportion of women who can comply with it is considerably smaller than the proportion of men who can comply with it, and which he cannot show to be justifiable irrespective of the sex of the person to whom it is applied and which is to her detriment because she cannot comply with it." Specific sections of the Act deal with housing (for sale or rent). Section 30, for example, says "it is unlawful for a person, in relation to premises in Great Britain of which he has power to dispose, to discriminate against a woman (1) in the terms on which he offers her the premises; or (2) by refusing her application for those premises; or (3) in his treatment of her in relation to any list of persons in need of premises of that description." Advice on the application of the Act as it relates to the provision of local authority services and premises is given in a D.O.E. circular: *Sex Discrimination Act 1975: Provisions affecting Local Government* (D.O.E. 1/78 and Welsh Office (W.O.) 3/78).

Reforms in the law have given women substantial gains. Later in this chapter we discuss the position of various groups of women according to marital status, and in Chapter 4 we consider how far these legal changes have been effective and how far they need supplementing either by further changes in the law or by better enforcement.

The effect of women's role on the design of housing
In the same way as the law has expressed traditional assumptions in regard to property and family life, so too have the provison and design of housing. In some ways it is not surprising that at any one time housing will reflect older social values since much of the housing in use may be over 100 years old. Fortunately, it has often been possible to adapt older forms of housing to newer forms of living and this process is going on all the time. Unfortunately, it seems likely that some modern forms, such as the tower block, will make adaptation much less easy. It is also regrettable that sometimes policy and practice for new building fail to take into account the changing social scene.

Even reports which in the past have been regarded as quite enlightened have in fact helped perpetuate outdated stereotypes. Thus the Parker Morris report *Homes for Today and Tomorrow,* when discussing family housing, said, "The first baby will mean that the mother begins to spend most of her time looking after the child and the house, and for several years, with further children coming along, the family will live with many interrupted nights, daytimes punctuated by rapid visits to the shops and by children's rests, and mealtimes after which the floor needs a good clean. . . . Soon they will all have started school, and some mothers take up part-time work."[12] And later talking about space for meals "The general pattern is for breakfast to be taken, often in relays, in the kitchen; for lunch, where the man of the house is often not present, to be taken there. . . ."[13]

This should be contrasted with the actual situation some years later when the *General Household Survey* (1976) showed that 60 per cent of married women with a child aged 5–9 and 26 per cent of married women with a child under 4 years, were working.[14] Also by this date 11 per cent of all families with dependent children were single parent families, compared with 8 per cent in 1971.[15]

The Parker Morris report was published in 1961 but the same kind of assumptions, i.e. that there will be two parents to provide for dependent children and that the wife will stay at home to look after them are still made. For example design guides still in use for planning family housing give a picture of family life with the mother always waiting on her family. The same kind of picture, when portrayed in children's books, is now under attack. And it is only fair to say that some of the early guidance, e.g. in the Dudley and Parker Morris reports, had the advantage of a good deal of evidence from women's organisations. Indeed the Dudley committee went out of its way to stress the particular evidence they had received from women's organisations.[16] From a design point of view it may not matter whether it is the man or the woman in the kitchen. It is the assumption that it will always be the woman which is so unhelpful to those who reject this kind of stereotyping.

Many of the complaints over design arise because women have traditionally spent more time in the home than men, particularly during the child rearing years. Some types of design are more unsuitable than others. The disadvantages for families of living in flats above ground level are well documented.[17] And government policies have been directed to advising local authorities to allocate them houses or ground floor accommodation, e.g. the Circular (D.O.E. 35/73 and W.O. 72/73) which accompanied Design Bulletin No. 27 *Children at Play*.

A report on a conference about women and housing co-operatives noted "Flexibility is not only needed externally but internally as well. When we talked about woman-defined architecture, we considered the value of impermanent, adjustable walls to permit scope for changing needs of women and growing children."[18] Later, when discussing the value of communal spaces, they said "We see the designs of our housing including features that cater for collective childcare. One woman at the conference, a single mother living at the top of a tower block along with other single mothers, told us of their experiences sharing the minding of children. Because of the nature of their individual flats with no common space, they have to continually shift their children from one place to another."[19]

Some have argued that one reason for poor designs is because so few women are involved in the related professions. "Architecture is a male-defined and male-dominated occupation" say Rights of Women.[20] Others hold that, while increasing the number of women in professions such as architecture will help, this is not the complete answer. Susan Jackson, an architect, suggests "The role of women as building users must be looked at more closely than just whether the housewife can supervise the children at play while she incessantly washes up. Each time a woman architect designs living accommodation she must ask the question 'why must all housing be geared towards the man who works and the woman who keeps house?'"[21] In Bath the Business and Professional Women's Club, in conjunction with the Bath Group of

Architects, mounted an exhibition devoted to the needs of women living alone[22] and the Feminist Design Collective in London are designing for a group of women clients. But these are rare occurrences.

The Feminist Group of the New Architecture Movement point out the effect of the design of estates as well as of internal design: "Women are isolated probably more effectively than ever before in any civilisation in history. We are boxed up with our children in high rise flats, surrounded by empty corridors and wastelands of empty space, imprisoned in tenement blocks or marooned in suburban semi-detached homes, surrounded by other people's hedges and gardens where neighbours hardly know each other."[23] Fortunately. there is increasing recognition (such as in designing for single people and the elderly) that there are different patterns of living and varying types of household. Women involved in architecture are increasingly questioning the traditional assumptions on which much design is based.

The emergence of a feminist critique of the internal and external design of housing is, however, still in its infancy. Much more thought, research and discussion is needed before a comprehensive view of this subject can be given.

We now go on to consider the housing chances of women as they are influenced by marital status, that is being single, married, separated or divorced, cohabiting or widowed. Those considered to be in special groups, such as the homeless, the elderly or those subject to violence are examined in the next chapter.

Single women

General

Many of the disadvantages single women suffer from apply to single men as well. Until recently single persons tended to be regarded by public authorities as a low priority group and those wanting to rent usually had to take their chance in the shrinking private sector. Those wanting to buy have found difficulties because building societies traditionally lend for family housing. There has been a lack of new accommodation because developers too (apart from the luxury flat market) have traditionally built family houses.

Over the last 20 years changes in social habits, corroborated by research, have made it clear that the single should no longer be regarded as a transient group. Recently building societies, developers and local authorities have begun to pay more attention to their needs.

Owner Occupation

Becoming an owner occupier usually involves negotiating a number of stages, each of which presents particular problems for the single woman. The fact that most women have lower incomes than men provides the first stumbling block. Saving enough money for a deposit, and then meeting mortgage payments, is difficult for a single person on a modest salary. The recently introduced government assistance under the *Home Purchase*

Assistance and Housing Corporation Guarantee Act 1978 for first time purchasers may prove helpful.

In the past women have often found it very difficult to obtain mortgages from building socieities, not only because of their low incomes, but because of discriminatory practices of the societies, such as asking for a male guarantor. But following the anti-discrimination legislation pressure has been exerted to change these practices. The Equal Opportunities Commission (E.O.C.) has recently found that most building societies now treat single men and women in the same way and apparently it is becoming easier for two women to get a joint mortgage. However this practice is not uniform and some women may still find it difficult. In many areas both building socieities and local authorities still look on 'unconventional households' as dubious mortgage risks.

Renting

Local authorities and housing associations are becoming more aware of the problems which single people face in housing and there is pressure from central government for their needs to be more generally considered. Some local authorities are building special accommodation. For example the London Borough of Hillingdon has a special block for single people and Leicester City Council has built a block of cluster-flats and bedsitter flats designed and appraised by the D.O.E. in Design Bulletin No. 33. Others are providing hostels and, in addition, offering property such as high rise blocks and difficult-to-let schemes to single people when others, such as families, find this housing unacceptable. Some housing associations are also providing schemes for the single.

However, schemes specially for single people are still an innovation. Many local authorities continue to give priority to families and may indeed have discriminatory rules against the single, such as not allocating housing to single people under 45. Much remains to be done before the general group of single people is satisfactorily housed.

The special position of single women with elderly dependants

There remains one particularly disadvantaged group of single people, those, usually women, who are caring for elderly relatives. Traditionally it has been the woman who has occupied this caring role and a growing number of studies have highlighted their problems. In particular the National Council for the Single Woman and her Dependants (N.C.S.W.D.) has taken up their cause. Founded in 1965 this organisation has among its aims increased domiciliary services and suitable housing. In a leaflet about aims and achievements it was estimated that in 1978 310,000 single women in Britain lived with parents over pensionable age. It was felt that women made great sacrifices to care for these elderly or infirm relatives at home, and many faced severe financial, social and emotional problems.

A research study *Single Women Caring for their Dependants* undertaken by the National Council was based on information gathered from among its members.[24] Replies were received from 360, of whom half had no paid employment at the time of the survey. One-fifth had given up their jobs to take up the caring role. Accommodation was identified as giving rise to major problems although the questionnaire did not apparently probe the type of problems encountered. Among examples given, however, were the difficulty of finding smaller accommodation, having to leave accommodation after the death of the dependant, poor facilities and dangerous features such as unsafe stairs.

Other difficulties faced by this group include cases "of a devoted daughter being rendered homeless following the division of family estate on death."[25] Not all local authorities are prepared to hand on a tenancy to the carer after the death of the dependant relative but there is now provision under the *Housing Bill 1980* for succession by people who have occupied the home as their only, or principal, home for the twelve months ending with the tenants' death. Housing problems like these, taken together with low income and lack of employment prospects, combine to give such women a bleak life both while they are carers and after their dependant has died.

The National Council is concerned with single *women* caring for dependants, and very little is known about the problems of single men in similar positions. The accepted domestic role of women in the past means that women still predominate in this role now. Will conditions improve if men accept a fairer share of the caring role?

Married women

General

In general the housing position of a married woman is 'protected' by her association with a male earner. If she is also employed she has a double advantage, for households with larger incomes tend to be those where the woman goes out to work. So although women, on average, earn less than men their contribution to the joint income can make a great deal of difference to the family's living standard. However, despite the legislation, there is still some discrimination in relation to the granting of mortgages, due to the perpetuation of assumptions that the man is the head of the household. Also when a marriage breaks down, or is ended by the death of the husband women face particular problems over their housing. (See later parts of this chapter.)

At one time only the income of the head of household (usually the man) was taken into account when mortgages were given. Now at least when a woman is married account is increasingly being taken of her income as well. But the E.O.C. showed that there was some discrimination against married women in respect to mortgages.[26] When a building society works out how much to lend on a joint mortgage they usually multiply the higher salary by a larger multiple – say 2½ and the lower by a smaller multiple – say ½, though some will add the two salaries together and double the total. It is usually the husband's salary which is taken as the main one. Indeed, in the E.O.C. sponsored research, it was found that in those cases where the wife earned more than her husband 36 per cent of branches of building societies in the sample still discriminated in some way against her. They often refused to take her income as the principal basis for calculating the mortgage. The main conclusion of the study was that where a wife earns more than her husband young couples are likely to be offered lower mortgages than where the earning capacity is reversed. Diane Balfe has suggested, with regard to local authorities lending practices, that they might "make a habit of referring to higher and lower wage-earners, rather than husbands and wives, when they are explaining mortgage policies to the public".[27] D.O.E. Circular 1/78 (para. 10) states "some local authorities may be reluctant to abandon long-established practices, based on the traditional assumptions of a married woman's economic dependency on her husband. The impact of the Act (*The Sex Discrimination Act*) on these matters is, however, unequivocal."

When property, whether owned or rented, is solely in the husband's name the woman may be in a less clear-cut position than if it were in their joint names. The Law Commission has recommended that husbands and wives should normally be equal owners of their homes.[28] They suggested statutory co-ownership of the matrimonial home, arguing that "The present law about the ownership of the matrimonial home during marriage is not only highly technical and sometimes uncertain in application, but inappropriate in substance."[29] They quote the findings of a social survey on the subject.[30] Married couples were asked: "Some people say that the home . . . should legally be jointly owned by the husband and wife irrespective of who paid for it. Do you agree or disagree with that?" 91 per cent of husbands and 94 per cent of wives who took part in the survey agreed with the proposition. It was also found that a majority of home-owning couples provided voluntarily for the co-ownership of their homes.

While joint ownership or joint tenancy of the home has advantages for women in making their position clear, there are some disadvantages if the marriage breaks up. For example, if the man leaves the woman becomes responsible for keeping up the payments. (See p. 15.)

Married women in tied accommodation

Most of the jobs that have accommodation provided are filled by men. The biggest categories are in agriculture, the police, the armed forces, the church, the prison department, the National Coal Board, British Rail and the fire service.[31] But many of these men have wives who share both the advantages and the disadvantages of this form of accommodation.

There are many advantages in living near a job, in many cases literally 'over the shop'. There may be no fares to pay and no stress in travelling. Many occupants pay no rent or only a nominal amount and this means more income to spend on other things. Some, too, like the clergy, live in larger or more grand accommodation than their salaries would buy although, with the cost of upkeep, this can be a distinct disadvantage.

On the other hand, few enjoy the security that tenants in the private rented sector have. One of the exceptions to this relates to agricultural workers who are now covered by the *Rent (Agriculture) Act 1976*. The rest are likely to lose their homes when they leave their jobs. They may also have to move around from area to area (e.g. servicemen) with little choice in the matter. When they retire they may find themselves without enough money to buy a home and without a residential qualification to apply for council accommodation although local authorities are increasingly making provision for this group.

Some women may also feel that their homes are only an extension of their husband's workplace and that they are 'on call' 24 hours a day. However, others, such as some clergy wives, welcome the chance to share in their husbands' jobs and feel that they can play a role too.

Particular difficulties may face a woman if her husband dies or leaves her. She will probably have to get out of her home within quite a short period of time. Jane Morton writing in *New Society* concluded "it is certainly not a system, in any form, that can be recommended unless operational effectiveness makes it unavoidable."[32] But there is in fact little evidence to show whether the people actually living in tied accommodation would wish to continue living in it or not if the opportunity arose. Indeed there is little evidence generally about tied accommodation and its occupants.

Shelter carried out one of the few pieces of research into tied accommodation and this covered those in the agricultural industry, in the coal mining industry, in the Armed Forces and generally in London. They concluded that because tied accommodation is by definition insecure it would be undesirable on those grounds alone. They also felt that in all types of insecure tenure there is the danger of sub-standard conditions not being remedied. They found "this danger to have become a fact in many instances of tied housing, which reinforces our opinion that tied housing is undesirable".[33]

Servicemen and their wives are one group of those in tied accommodation who have received a certain amount of publicity. Miss Janet Fookes, M.P. reported some of their arrangements to the Equal Opportunities Commission. She said that service regulations allowed husbands unilaterally to declare themselves estranged from their wives. The wives thus became illegal occupants of their married quarters and this was "discrimination against women of the worst kind."[34] Polly Toynbee has also taken up the cause of servicemen's wives and their accommodation.[35] The Ministry of Defence set up a study *The Pay and Conditions of Service* to examine, among other matters, accommodation, family separation, house purchase and fringe benefits.

Women whose marriages break down

General

In the past, major housing difficulties have faced women whose marriages have broken down. Inadequate provision and lack of legal safeguards have caused women to remain in marriages which are unsatisfactory and often forced them to expose themselves or their children to physical or mental cruelty. Many still do not realise the full extent of the rights which they now have, and in particular that they may be able to remain in the family home whether it is rented or owner occupied. There are certain principles which a court normally considers when dividing up property. The *Matrimonial Homes Act 1967* recognises the right of a spouse to occupy the matrimonial home but, as the Law Commission pointed out, "The right to occupy may be of little value unless there is a corresponding right to retain possession of the household goods."[36] A scheme was suggested in this report to protect the use and enjoyment of these household goods.

Increasingly, however, in recent years the courts have been considering as paramount the need of children to have a home and giving this much more consideration in the property settlement. The legislation in this field is complicated and practical guidance cannot be given here. Good general advice, however, is available from recent publications such as Maureen Leevers and Pat Thynne's *A Woman's Place* published by Shelter Housing Aid Centre (S.H.A.C.), Manchester Law Centre's Women's Handbook No. 2 *Getting your own home* and D.O.E.'s *One-Parent Families: A Guide to Housing Aid*.

Although much has been done to improve the situation it remains the case that the breakdown of a marriage tends to depress, at least for a time, either one or both of the partner's housing prospects. The home has to be allocated to one or the other or, if there are no children, if is often split between the two. Incomes which supported one home have to support two and, though in time other households may be formed, many people can find themselves in severe difficulty. These difficulties are exacerbated by housing shortage. Some public authorities for example will not consider rehousing either party (unless there is violence) until there is a legal separation or divorce.

Owner Occupation

In the event of a breakdown in the marriage it may be easier for the woman to remain in the home if it is in the joint names of husband and wife. In a survey of married couples and formerly married couples in 1971 it was found that 52 per cent of owner occupier couples had the home in their joint names, 42 per cent in the husband's name and 5 per cent in the wife's name.[37]

But even where the husband owns the home the woman may have an interest in it. Further than that she may become the sole owner. A Court of Appeal decided that where an order had been made for the sale of the matrimonial home when the youngest child was 17 "and the division of the net proceeds of sale between the spouses in equal shares did not produce a satisfactory result in a case where the wife's share in the proceeds would be completely inadequate to enable her to acquire alternative accommodation. . . . The fair way of dealing with the case, taking into account the needs of both parties, was to transfer the house to the wife absolutely and to reduce the periodical payments for the children to a nominal amount."[38]

Married women now have many property rights even when the home is in the husband's name, including a right to remain there until the court makes a property settlement. The husband can, for example, be stopped from selling the home before the settlement is made, and the woman cannot be evicted until a court order is made against her. More details can be found in Maureen Leevers and Pat Thynne's *A Woman's Place.*

Paying off the mortgage can also be a problem for a woman, particularly if she is suddenly left on her own through the desertion or death of her husband. A number of studies have drawn attention to the plight of such women.[39] And a growing number of articles and pamphlets such as Jo Tunnard's *Women and Housing – owner occupation* for the Child Poverty Action Group (C.P.A.G.) in 1978 and Jo Tunnard and Clare Whately's *Rights Guide for Home Owners* for C.P.A.G. and S.H.A.C. in 1979 both give advice and show how the position has improved for this group. The Supplementary Benefits Commission (S.B.C.) can help those on supplementary benefit by paying the interest on the mortgage and in certain cases an allowance for repairs and for the insurance of the home. Maintaining the house in good repair may be as big a problem as paying the mortgage, but some help is available through the local authority and more if the property is in a Housing Action Area or General Improvement Area.[40]

Liability for rates is an interesting issue. The husband is usually regarded as being in rateable occupation when the spouses live together. He may also be liable on desertion too. One writer has said that up until divorce a husband who deserted his wife and left her in the matrimonial home in which he had some interest which entitled him to allow her to occupy it "will find it difficult to avoid liability as rateable occupier despite his physical absence from the premises."[41]

Financial and other difficulties which may be faced by single parents are described in more detail in the next chapter.

Renting

Because of the decline in the private rented sector the majority of women who rent are likely to be in council accommodation. Some move to this sector. Alan Holmans says "The higher proportion of divorced or separated women householders who are local authority tenants suggests that in a significant number of instances marital breakdown leads to a move from owner occupation to renting . . .".[42] Between 1967 and 1975 the number of households receiving supplementary benefit in local authority tenancies who were women with dependent children nearly trebled. This is far more than could be attributed to higher divorce rates or more desertions and separations nationally. So local authorities were providing accommodation for an increasing proportion of widows, divorced and deserted women with children.[43]

It seems that local authorities are also now becoming increasingly aware of the advantages of couples being granted a joint tenancy.[44] However, this may not be an unmitigated blessing for a woman for, if her husband leaves, she may be held responsible for any rent arrears. It is interesting that in the circular on one-parent families *Housing for One-Parent Families* it is stated "Some joint tenancies are granted by local authorities to couples, though the Finer

Committee, having considered their value, did not recommend that they should be introduced generally."[45] Once in the property, there has in the past been less statutory security compared with people who rented privately. However, in practice, evictions have been rare and the new security of tenure given to council tenants, although it will not *stop* evictions, may help make tenants feel less vulnerable.

The question of who retains the council tenancy if a marriage fails was discussed briefly in the Cullingworth report.[46]. The committee said that they had been assured by many local authorities that they followed a policy of "tenancy follows the children." Some local authorities have insisted on the wife obtaining a court order against her husband before any transfer of tenancy can be made.[47] And there may be problems over the transfer which can cause much distress and insecurity.

Cohabitees

The rights of cohabitees are still being fought out. For instance, the Law Commission on *Family Law and the Matrimonial Home,* previously referred to, only dealt with husbands and wives. As Robin Young commented in *The Times* (15 June 1978) "The rights of so-called common-law wives and their male counterparts are not dealt with, as they are held to raise problems that go far beyond property issues." However, in a recent case a woman who consented to the adoption of her illegitimate daughter at the insistence of a divorced man, and lived with him for four years as his common law wife, was held to be entitled to provision out of his estate under the *Inheritance (Provision for Family and Dependants) Act, 1975.*[48]

Maggie Rae has pointed out that, while English law does not recognise cohabitation as a legal relationship, there has been growing recognition in recent years that it may be unfair to view the relationships between cohabitees on a strictly legal basis. She says "Although the developments made in the law relating to cohabitees have been only tentative they have affected both the right to occupy property and rights of ownership over it."[49] The law has intervened in certain circumstances to give a cohabitee who is not the legal owner or joint owner an interest in property where there has been violence. However the rights of unmarried women as far as property protection go are not as great as those of married women. The National Women's Aid Federation (N.W.A.F.) pose the question "But how, if a new system of law is established, can one avoid basing it on the traditional assumptions of married family life and the woman's dependent position in the family?"[50]

Cohabitees are not in a strong position as far as renting is concerned. For those in the council sector it is up to the local authority whether it grants a tenancy to the woman when the tenancy is in the man's name. But the position is complicated partly because one tenancy has to be terminated legally, by notice or surrender, before another can be granted. Where the tenancy is in the woman's name there should be fewer problems but if the man will not leave proceedings for trespass may have to be taken.

Widows
Widows may also have housing problems, some of which may be to do with income. In particular, lack of the main breadwinner's income may mean that mortgage repayments and even rent become difficult to sustain. The problem may be particularly acute if the woman has young children and is not able, or does not want, to work. Not all women know that the Supplementary Benefits Commission can pay interest on the mortgage. Older widows are (in common with widowers) more likely to be local authority tenants than are married couples. Alan Holmans suggests that "Elderly widows and widowers are more likely to be in the over-75, or over-85, groups than are elderly married people; and also, being without a husband or wife to care for them, are more likely to need special accommodation."[51] Partly as a result of special accommodation being built "Widowhood and divorce appear in a considerable number of instances to be the occasion of moves to a local authority tenancy by older one person households."[52]

Conclusions
What is striking about this examination of the effect of marital status on women's position in housing is the growing recognition of their disadvantaged position. There have been advances on nearly every front: legally, in policy, in practice and through changes in attitudes. But, as many of the studies indicate, there is still some way to go until there is a real measure of equality.

References
1. J. McNamara and S. F. Wemple. 'Sanctity and Power: The Dual Pursuit of Medieval Women' in *Becoming Visible: Women in European History* by R. Bridenthal and C. Koonz, Houghton Miffin Co., U.S.A., 1977.
2. Government Social Survey. *A Handbook for Interviewers* by J. Atkinson, H.M.S.O., 1968, p. 117.
3. F. Engels. *The Origin of the Family, Private Property and the State,* International Publishers Co. Inc., 1942.
4. Office of Population Censuses and Surveys (O.P.C.S.). *Family Formation* by K. Dunnell, H.M.S.O., 1979, p. 84.
5. *E.O.C. Bulletin.* Winter 1978–79, p. 9.
6. Central Statistical Office (C.S.O.). *Social Trends* No. 10, H.M.S.O., 1979, p. 84.
7. *Ibid.*
8. O.P.C.S. *Family Formation, op. cit.,* pp. 86–87.
9. *Ibid.* p. 87.
10. *Ibid.* p. 22.
11. *Ibid.*
12. Ministry of Housing and Local Government (M.H.L.G.). *Homes for Today and Tomorrow* (the Parker Morris report), H.M.S.O., 1961, pp. 8–9.
13. *Ibid.* p. 10.
14. *E.O.C. Bulletin, op. cit.,* p. 19.
15. *Ibid.* p. 17.
16. Ministry of Health (M.O.H.). Sub-committee of the C.H.A.C., *Design of Dwellings,* H.M.S.O., 1944, p. 8.

17. A useful summary of research is given in D.O.E., Housing Development Directorate, Occasional Paper 1/75, *The Social Effects of living off the ground,* H.M.S.O., 1975.
18. *Scoop.* The Newsletter of the Society of Co-operative Dwellings, No. 6, 6/78, p. 16.
19. *Ibid.*
20. Rights of Women. *Women and Housing* paper, p. 2. Presented at the Shelter Conference, July, 1978.
21. *Slate.* Issue 8, July/August, 1978, p. 13.
22. M. Withers. 'A Place of her own', *Architect and Building News,* 19.6.69, pp. 48–52.
23. Leaflet produced prior to a weekend school, March, 1979.
24. National Council for the Single Woman and her Dependants. *Single Women caring for their Dependants,* N.C.S.W.D., 1978. See also earlier accounts of two smaller studies, one in Woolwich and one in Southampton. N.C.S.W.D. *The Single Woman with Dependants,* July, 1979.
25. R. Arnold. 'The inequitable treatment for those caring for elderly or infirm relatives', *Poverty* No. 28, Spring, 1974.
26. E.O.C. *'It's not your business, it's how the Society works',* the experience of married applicants for joint mortgages, a report of a survey carried out by the Consumers Association Survey Unit, 1978.
27. D. Balfe. 'How to make home loans to women – legally', *Local Government Chronicle,* 21.9.79, pp. 996–97.
28. The Law Commission. No. 86. *Family Law – Third report on Family Property: The Matrimonial Home (Co-ownership and occupation rights) and Household Goods,* H.M.S.O., 1978.
29. *Ibid.* p. 3.
30. J. Todd and L. Jones. *Matrimonial Property,* Social Survey Division, O.P.C.S., H.M.S.O., 1972.
31. M.H.L.G. *Council Housing Purposes, Procedures and Priorities,* (the Cullingworth report), H.M.S.O., 1969, pp. 74–76 and M. Constable. *Tied Accommodation,* Shelter, 1974.
32. J. Morton. 'Tied to the job', *New Society,* 11.4.74.
33. M. Constable. *op. cit.,* p. 29. See also S. Schifferes. *The Forgotten Problem,* Shelter, 1980.
34. *The Times,* 4.10.78.
35. *The Guardian,* 6.11.78.
36. The Law Commission, *op. cit.* p. 5.
37. J. Todd and L. Jones, *op. cit.*
38. Hanlon *v.* Hanlon. Reported in *The Times,* 20.10.77. But the position has been further complicated by a decision that if the house is sold legal aid may have to be paid back. *The Times,* 2.5.80.
39. For example:
J. Tunnard. *No Father, No Home?,* Poverty Pamphlet 28, C.P.A.G., 1976.
J. Tunnard. 'The Mortgage Vows', *Roof,* November, 1978, back page.
V. Karn, in 'Pity the Poor Home Owners', discusses some of the problems of low income owners which draws some conclusions from a study in Birmingham, *Roof,* January, 1979, pp. 10–14.
40. Details of the sort of help available to the elderly and other groups are discussed by A. Tinker and J. White, *Housing Review,* May/June, 1979.
41. G. Miller, 'Rateable occupation of the matrimonial home', *Local Government Chronicle,* 3.11.78, pp. 1196–97.
42. C.S.O. *Social Trends* No. 9, H.M.S.O., 1978, p. 13.
43. D.O.E. *Housing Policy.* Technical Volume Part III, H.M.S.O., 1977, p. 12.
44. *Municipal Review.* December 1976, Supplementary Report of the Housing Committee on the *Sex Discrimination Act,* paras. 13–15.
45. D.O.E. Circular 78/77 (W.O. 123/77), *Housing for One-Parent Families,* H.M.S.O., 1977, para. 21.
46. M.H.L.G. The Cullingworth report, *op. cit.*
47. D. Yates. 'The Council House as the Matrimonial Home', in *Social Welfare Law,* Issue No. 1, 1978.

48. Law report 17.11.78. C. A. and Another *v.* C. C. and Others. Reported in *The Times*, 18.11.78.
49. M. Rae. 'Cohabitees and Property Rights', *Roof,* Housing Advice Notes, No. 17, September, 1978, pp. 157–78.
50. N.W.A.F., National Council for Civil Liberties and Rights of Women. *Women and Housing*, papers produced for a conference on battered women and refuges, 10.6.78, p. 8.
51. In *Social Trends* No. 9, *op. cit.,* p. 14.
52. D.O.E. *Housing Policy.* Technical Volume Part III, *op. cit.,* p. 11.

CHAPTER 3

Disadvantaged Groups

Introduction

In the previous chapter we have considered the effect of law and marital status on women's access to housing and also the particular opportunities and disadvantages of various groups according to their marital status. In this chapter the position of those in what are officially defined as disadvantaged groups will be described.

There is a high degree of agreement in official pronouncements as to which

Table 3.1
Groups considered to be in particular housing need

	By the Cullingworth Committee[1]	By the Housing Corporation[2]	By the D.O.E. *Housing Policy* Green Paper[3]
Single people	×	×	×
Elderly people	×	×	×
Homeless people	×	×	×
Coloured people/ethnic minorities	(coloured people)	×	(ethnic minorities)
Single parent families	—	×	×
Battered women	—	—	×
Students	×	×	×
Large families	×	×	—
Lower income households	—	×	×
The physically disabled	—	×	×
The mentally ill and mentally handicapped	—	×	×
Mobile workers	—	×	×

1. M.H.L.G. *Council Housing Purposes, Procedures and Priorities*, H.M.S.O., 1969, Ch. 8, Some important needs and Ch. 9, Housing coloured people.
2. The Housing Corporation. *The selection of tenants by housing associations for subsidised schemes*, Circular 1/75, The Housing Corporation, 1975.
3. D.O.E. *Housing Policy. A Consultative Document*, Cmnd. 6851, H.M.S.O., 1977, Ch. 12, Individual Housing Needs.

groups are disadvantaged. The Cullingworth Report,[1] The D.O.E. *Housing Policy* Green Paper[2] and the advice given by the Housing Corporation[3] to associations which they fund are the sources which we have used. Table 3.1 shows the degree of consensus between them.

The three lists define 12 groups considered to be in special housing need. The groups are not mutually exclusive. An elderly person may be single, a battered wife may become a single parent, and someone who is homeless may be from an ethnic minority. Of the 12 groups mentioned three (ethnic minorities, students and mobile workers) have more men than women, two (single people, excluding the elderly, and large families) have evenly balanced numbers, seven (the elderly, the physically disabled, the mentally disordered, single parents, battered women, those officially accepted as homeless, and lower income households) have more women than men.

In this chapter we concentrate on those groups which have more women than men, but we conclude with a few points about women in some of the other disadvantaged groups. There are two groups (the elderly and the physically disabled) where the higher proportion of women is due largely to physical factors such as living longer and being more susceptible to certain diseases which cause disability. The problems they face are those common to most other members of the groups, though women may be subject to additional disdavantages. In the other five groups the predominance of women is due to more complex legal, economic or social causes.

The elderly

The largest group of disadvantaged people in which women are the majority is the *elderly*.

Of the 7.8 million people over the age of 65 in Great Britain in 1977, 3 million were men and 4.8 million were women.[4] The great imbalance between the sexes is in the upper age ranges: compared with men there are twice as many women in the 75–84 age group and three times as many aged 85 and over. The life expectation at birth of a man in 1951 was 66.2 years and in 1977 69.5. The life expectation for a woman at birth in 1951 was 71.2 years and in 1977 75.7. The gap between the sexes has therefore widened. The greater number of women is important because they are more likely to be physically handicapped than men. Women, for example, are almost twice as likely to have arthritis or rheumatism than men of similar ages.[5]

Numbers, too, will continue to increase. It is estimated that between 1977 and 1991 the number of over 65s in Great Britain will go up from 7.8 million to 8.3 million, and again the major increase will be in the older age group. While the 60–64s will decline by 7 per cent and the 65–74s by 4 per cent, the 75–84s will increase by 20 per cent and the over 85s by 42 per cent.

It is, of course, as dangerous to generalise about this group as about any other. To many old people housing presents no problem. But for many others the combination of a small income and increasing disability makes it difficult for them to manage.

Where then do this group live and what are some of their problems? Approximately 89 per cent live in ordinary accommodation either owned by themselves, rented, or in other households. About five per cent live in their own home in sheltered housing and six per cent live in some form of institutional care – mainly old people's homes or hospitals.[6]

Of those in private households many live alone and often face difficulties when they become ill and need help. And in the next few years the number of those living alone will go up still further. In the *Housing Policy* Green Paper it was stated that an increase of nearly one million is projected between 1971 and 1986 in the number of men and women above retirement age living as one person households. But the main difficulty with which this group has to contend is the poorer accommodation that they tend to occupy. For example, a recent large national survey *(The National Dwelling and Housing Survey)* showed that the elderly lacked basic amenities such as an indoor w.c., bathroom and hot water to a much greater extent than other groups.[7]

Homes may become increasingly difficult to manage as stairs become hard to negotiate, and repairs expensive to get done. The home may also be larger than is necessary. Underoccupation is not an easy subject to raise with some elderly people as was discovered by the 1976 O.P.C.S. survey *The Elderly at Home*, when it was found not to be possible to put a question on this point. The pilot survey found that it caused too much worry to the respondents.

The remaining 11 per cent who are in sheltered housing and residential care are nearly all women. While there has been no national survey of tenants in sheltered housing all the studies to date indicate that about 70–80 per cent of tenants are women.[8] And at the time of the 1971 census there were nearly three times as many women in residential care as men.

The five per cent of elderly people who live in sheltered housing have many advantages. They have their own independent flat or bungalow and a warden on hand for emergencies. But they can still have problems. A bedsitting room flat or a flat with only one bedroom usually means that much-loved furniture has to be left behind. Schemes are not always sited conveniently. But for those who enjoy living in groups with people of their own age this sort of living arrangement seems very satisfactory. From existing evidence it seems that over half the tenants stay there until they die.[9] It remains to be seen whether satisfaction with schemes will be the same when the proportion of frail, elderly tenants (most of whom will be women) becomes much higher as schemes age. Already a number of problems are arising.

Elderly women living in institutional care can face different problems of their own. To begin with some may be there merely because they lack suitable accommodation. There is evidence for this in numerous surveys. The buildings may be old and decrepit. Although many of the old poor law homes have been taken out of use there are still unsatisfactory former workhouses or other adapted buildings in use. Some people may feel acutely the loss of freedom and dignity. Staff attitudes may not be conducive to happy living. The Personal Social Services Council in *Residential Care Reviewed* (1976) has discussed some of these issues.

The physically disabled

The *physically disabled* are a difficult group to define because of the different degrees of disablement, but using almost any criteria women predominate. It has been estimated that one woman in 11 is physically impaired (that is, lacks part or all of a limb or has a defective limb or has a defective organ or mechanism of the body which stops or limits getting about, working or self-care) compared with one man in 15.[10] In 1971 it was estimated that there were 1.2 million men and 1.8 million women in Great Britain with some impairment, living in private households. Men predominated among the under 50s and women in the age groups above. Not everyone, however, who is disabled is necessarily at a disadvantage. It is when there is disadvantage or restriction of activity caused by disability that there is handicap. But handicap and disablement do tend to be terms which are used interchangeably.

Estimated numbers of those very severely, severely or appreciably handicapped in Great Britain in 1971 were 365,000 men and 763,000 women. Two-thirds of these were over 65 and for this age group there were more than twice as many women as men. For those even more disabled and in wheelchairs it was estimated that in England and Wales there were 113,000 in 1973.[11] From these figures it is estimated that women predominate – 2.7 of every 1,000 population are wheelchair users compared with 1.8 per 1,000 for men. Sally Sainsbury also found a predominance of women in her study *Registered as Disabled*.[12] More than three-fifths of her sample were women.

There are two main reasons for the predominance of women. One is that the elderly form a high proportion of the physically disabled and women outnumber men at this age. Secondly, women seem more prone than men to certain disabilities such as arthritis.

The housing problems of the physically disabled vary in the same way as their disabilities. The blind, the deaf, those in wheelchairs and those on renal dialysis have quite different needs. Some evidence about the housing conditions of this group is to be found in the second part of *Handicapped and Impaired in Great Britain*.[13] In general, their accommodation was no better and no worse than that for the rest of the population. However, 10 per cent of people were unable to use part of their accommodation because of some disability. Stairs were usually the main limiting factor and 8 per cent of impaired persons sometimes or always slept in their living room, usually because their disability made use of bedrooms difficult. About one in four of the sample would have liked to have moved.

One ideal to be aimed for was outlined by a working party on housing set up by the Central Council for the Disabled. Their report stated "A disabled person and his family should not be at any disadvantage as a result of his disability, in seeking to obtain the type of accommodation he desires, in the area of his choice. He should be able to live as independently as he desires within the limitations of his handicap [and . . .] should not be placed at a social or housing disadvantage on account of his physical disabilities."[14]

The location of their housing is clearly important for the physically handicapped. Ease of access to shops, post office, doctor, chemist and other amenities is likely to allow greater independence. Some local authorities have found, for example, that an adapted house locally may well be more acceptable than a purpose-built one some miles away.

The mentally disordered

The *mentally disordered* were not one of the groups singled out by the Cullingworth Committee as being disadvantaged in housing. However in both the *Housing Policy* Green Paper and the Housing Corporation circular it was considered that this group had particular housing needs. (See Table 3.1.)

Mental disorder covers two separate conditions – mental illness and mental handicap. Among the mentally ill, that is people with psychiatric illnesses, women predominate. For example, in a study of mental illness and the psychiatric services Bransby estimated that one in six women and one in nine men are likely to be admitted to a psychiatric hospital once in their lifetime.[15] And in the same study he concluded "A finding common to most surveys of psychiatric morbidity and those of self-reported symptoms is the greater prevalence among women than men." Some feminists argue that some of these problems are male defined and male induced.

The mentally handicapped are those with arrested or incomplete development of the mind, commonly described as subnormal. Their numbers are more difficult to estimate. The Department of Health and Social Security (D.H.S.S.) admit that "We do not know precisely the prevalence of mental handicap nor the number of mentally handicapped people who require particular forms of help."[16] In view of this lack of factual information about the mentally handicapped this chapter will be concerned only with the mentally ill.

Some mentally ill people will need to spend time in residential care, but difficulties arise when it is appropriate for them to lead more independent lives. Many will, of course, go straight home but this is not the right solution for everyone. Difficulties can arise, as D.H.S.S. state in *Better Services for the Mentally Ill:* "Where for example a mother's illness has in part been precipitated by the stresses arising from the housing in which she was living, a return to the situation which proved too much for her before may prejudice her chance of a full recovery or even cause a recurrence of her illness."[17] Nor will all patients have families to return to. What is required is variety of provision, from hostels which offer a good deal of support to independent accommodation.

Many mentally ill women will either remain in their own homes or will return to them after treatment in a psychiatric hospital. Others, however, may want to make a fresh start when they leave institutional care. Usually specially designed housing is not needed. Many will be able to live without special support in ordinary housing. But if they do need some support, a housing authority can provide cluster flats or bedsitter accommodation, together with any necessary support from the social services; or else the housing authority can provide ordinary flats and houses to serve as group homes, with the social services again providing support. People who need the mutual support of living together in a small group can also sometimes live together as one household. Examples of councils providing accommodation where a small group of discharged patients can live together have recently been described.[18]

Another alternative which is just beginning to be developed is boarding out. Attempts are being made to find people who will take in as a lodger a person who has been mentally ill. M.I.N.D. in *Room to Let* in 1976 argued that each local authority should employ an officer with specific responsibility for finding accommodation for discharged psychiatric patients. Hostels are another option. Elizabeth Durkin describes these hostels as having two main aims. First to rehabilitate their residents and second to compensate them for their lack of social contacts and relationships in the community.[19] She maintains that thought must be given to the aims, functions and effectiveness of different types of social organisation. But there is some scepticism about how far hostels do achieve rehabilitation.

Single parents

The majority of *single parent families* consist of women bringing up children alone. Of the estimated 750,000 single parent families with dependent children in Great Britain in 1976 88 per cent were women and 12 per cent men.[20] These proportions have not changed since 1971, but in 1976 there were more single and divorced among the women and fewer who were widows or separated. Single parent families constituted 8 per cent of all families with dependent children in 1971 and 11 per cent in 1976.

These figures give a snapshot at a particular moment in time. Many more parents and children will have been members of single parent families at some point in their lives. Nor must it be forgotten that in practice many more parents (usually women) may be bringing up children single-handed when their spouse is away from home for a long time, perhaps on construction work on an oil rig, or in the forces, or in prison. Looking to the future, it seems likely that numbers may increase unless the growing trend for marriages to break down is reversed. The Department of the Environment estimate that the number of single parent households (this includes households containing sons or daughters of *any* age) will grow from 1.2 million in 1976 to nearly 1.3 million in 1986 in England and Wales.[21]

Many women then are likely to come into this group at some time. What are the housing problems they may face? The main source of information is the report of the Committee on *One-Parent Families* (the Finer Committee) which was published in 1974.[22] It found that although not all one parent families had housing problems many had. There was an unmistakable and pronounced incidence of hardship and disadvantage found in the group as a whole. One of the main reasons why this group could not compete on equal terms with others for housing was found to be lack of money. Poor living conditions were generally acknowledged to be one of the great disadvantages suffered by this group. Standards of room occupancy, household amenities and rooms and beds shared were found to be worse for one parent families than for two parent ones. Numbers are difficult to assess. We know that one quarter of both male and female single parent households share with others,[23] and it is also forecast that the numbers will rise. These households are technically known as 'concealed' and it is not known how many would wish to have their own homes. This lack of independent accommodation was a matter for comment by the Finer Committee. They said that "the biggest single difference between the housing circumstances of one and two parent families is the very high proportion of one-parent families who share a home, usually with close relatives." This varies with marital status. Unmarried mothers are more likely, and widows less likely, to be sharing a home.

There was also evidence that fatherless families – with the exception of widows – moved more often than other households. This not only caused problems in regard to changes of school and lack of social contacts but also was possibly the reason for failure to get a place on a local authority housing list where residential qualifications are required. Another problem is the possibility of becoming homeless. One third of families accepted as homeless are one-parent families. This group will be considered in more detail later.

Research, such as that carried out by the Child Poverty Action Group (for example, Jo Tunnard's 1976 study *No Father, No Home?*) has corroborated much of the earlier evidence. However, the evidence produced about conditions prior to 1974 has to be set alongside the much greater attention now paid to this group and the fact that some of the Finer Committee recommendations have been implemented. The D.O.E. Circular *Housing For One-Parent Families* (1977) lists some of these. The view was expressed in this circular that one-parent families do not generally require accommodation which is different from that needed by other families. They should receive effective parity of treatment in housing matters alongside two parent families. Local authorities were advised to consider applications on the basis of housing need and "to review their policies to ensure that any discrimination referred to in recommendation 148 is brought quickly to an end". Recommendation 148 of the Finer Committee referred to the practice of considering single parents as "less deserving". This advice about treating single parent families as two parent ones makes good management sense because a large proportion of single parents subsequently marry. If the accommodation is suitable for two adults at the outset then it saves the upheaval of a move when the single parent marries or cohabits.

Very young unmarried mothers who may not be able to cope with running a full sized home were considered an exceptional case and it was thought that they might benefit from special housing schemes with the possibility of extra facilities such as communal space for use as a nursery, crêche or playgroup. The circular also included support for the *Domestic Violence and Matrimonial Proceedings Act, 1976* and for the *Housing (Homeless Persons) Act, 1977*. Subsequently, a booklet was issued in 1978 giving advice on help with housing (D.O.E. *One-Parent Families: A Guide to Housing Aid.*) The D.O.E. Housing Services Advisory Group have also made a number of recommendations in their report *The Housing of One-Parent Families* in 1978. The latter recommended a number of things, including abolition of residential qualifications, equal treatment with two parent families in the quality of housing and area if they are offered a tenancy and single parent families to be given the same size accommodation as two parent families with the same number of children.

Attention is currently being focused on the question of whether the Finer recommendations are being carried out. For example, a local authority may have changed its waiting list policy on bedroom allocation but in the case of families rehoused as homeless may still give them one bedroom less (e.g. rehousing a mother with one child in a one bedroom flat). Since the largest proportion of rehousing may be of homeless people this will in effect negate the recommended policy. Also rehousing as homeless persons may tend to congregate single parent families on difficult-to-let or stigmatised estates along with other 'disadvantaged groups'.

In two areas it does seem that the position of single parents is improving. Local authorities appear to be accepting more of this group and more advice is being given to women in this position who own their own homes. Looking at these points in greater detail it does appear from evidence presented in D.O.E. *Housing Policy* that local authorities are filling the gap left by the shrinking of the private rented sector. This is important because single parent families have in the past relied more on private rented accommodation than many other households.

Single parent families who live in a home with a mortgage face another range of problems but, again, there does seem now to be a greater appreciation of these difficulties and of what can be done to help. Jo Tunnard, who has done research on this group, reported in a paper on *Women and Housing: Owner Occupation* for the Child Poverty Action Group "They have a common worry: they are terrified at the thought of losing their home and of being forced to move with their children to inferior quality housing". Many single parents do not realise that they can keep a mortgage going. But in 1975 there were 21,000 single parent families on supplementary benefit living in mortgaged property. Jo Tunnard, on behalf of the Child Poverty Action Group, has carried out research into fatherless families living in homes with mortgages and has given advice to many single parents in this position. In answer to the question "Can a mortgage be sustained from a low income?" her answer is "yes, if borrowers and their advisors make the best use of welfare benefits and tax allowances, mortgage arrangements and property, and matrimonial law". It is claimed by C.P.A.G. that ignorance is a major cause of single parents failing to keep their homes. The booklet by D.O.E. previously referred to (*One-Parent Families: A Guide to Housing Aid*) should help.

Battered women

Battered women form another category of people recognised as being disadvantaged. In the interest of equality perhaps the term should be battered spouses, because men too can be physically and mentally abused. The men, the batterers, also need help. Erin Pizzey says "But the violent men of today, whose families come to us, are trapped inside their pattern of violent behaviour". She says that they too need a way out, or they will marry again and the whole pattern be repeated.[24] Having said that, however, by far the most pressing problem is that of the battered woman, and Erin Pizzey has done much to bring the subject to the notice of the public. In 1971 she founded Chiswick Women's Aid in a house which became a refuge for battered women. Growing public concern was evident in 1974–75 when a Select Committee of the House of Commons was set up on Violence in Marriage. Since the early 1970s the National Women's Aid Federation have further publicised the plight of this particular group. However, it is salutary to remember that the problem is not new and it is ironical that another Select Committee looked into the problems and causes of 'wife torturing' as far back as 1878.

In general, a number of the housing problems of this group are similar to those of single parent families (see previous section). And members of this group are at risk of being homeless.

Some of the problems may be specific to this group and research being undertaken by the National Women's Aid Federation and sponsored by the D.O.E. may help to give further information. The first stage involves gathering information about refuges and the second includes a study of the battered women's view of their housing needs. In the short term, the need of the battered woman is for immediate protection and accommodation away from her spouse. A number may escape to family or friends. However, some women feel safer in a community and find it helpful to be with a group of women who have suffered in the same way. For them a refuge may be the answer. Many refuges are run by local voluntary women's aid groups and most are affiliated to the National Women's Aid Federation.

The value of refuges is borne out by a study carried out for the D.H.S.S. by Jan Pahl who listed the needs of battered women as protection, accommodation, support and advice. A multi-functional refuge, "offering different help to different women, and different help to the same woman at different times during her stay" is how she sees their role.[25] One of the conclusions of a study by Maureen Leevers in *Violence in Marriage* for S.H.A.C. was that more Women's Aid Centres were needed. Jan Pahl has pointed out some of the inherent drawbacks in the management style of many refuges, and even good ones may not be right for all battered women. In 1977 it was held that "Women's aid groups encounter many problems in finding properties suitable for use as refuges and in meeting the costs of essential repairs, conversion, renovation and maintenance".[26] Subsequent research by the National Women's Aid Federation has found that refuges "were usually providing a service with little financial support and in unsuitable and overcrowded accommodation. Lack of facilities for children were particularly marked. However, it was clear from the interviews with battered women that their need for refuge was considerable and that they saw refuges as an important and growing escape route from domestic violence".[27]

Long term solutions have to differ according to differing needs. Some women may continue to want the support of other women and live in a co-operative or share a home. Many will marry again or cohabit. Others may want their own home. For some, this may be literally the desire to return to their own home. They may need help, perhaps a court order, to do this but the *Domestic Violence and Matrimonial Proceedings Act 1976* has given additional powers to the courts and simplified the procedure. It applies both to married couples and to a man and woman who live together in the same household. Where there is domestic violence the Act makes it easier for the woman to remain in the home. It also allows a spouse to obtain an injunction to exclude the other from the family home. The N.W.A.F. has some reservations about the working of the Act and is monitoring its working.

Other women may want a fresh start and a council tenancy may well be their only hope since there is now little privately rented accommodation. Although there is still a long way to go more councils are recognising the needs of battered women. The London Borough of Haringey, for example, in a report in 1978 on *Women and Housing* prepared by the Borough Housing Officer made a number of recommendations, including one that sympathetic consideration be given where women are eligible for rehousing for them, if they wished, to be near other women similarly rehoused from refuges. Other recommendations included no action for rent arrears on the woman if she is forced to leave home as a result of violence.

Battered women who want to get right away from their original surroundings may find it difficult to get accepted without a residential qualification for accommodation by a council. However, not every council insists on this, and the recommendation that local authorities should end the practice of imposing residential or other qualifications for inclusion on their housing list would also help if fully implemented.

Homeless women

Women also figure strongly among the homeless. Actual numbers are difficult to come by, not least because there is no generally accepted definition of homelessness. Shelter, a national organisation concerned with preventing homelessness, holds that "many families living in substandard housing or separated or sharing with relatives are just as 'homeless' as those in officially provided accommodation".[28] In the *Housing (Homeless Persons) Act, 1977* the definition is a much narrower one. In defining the specific duties of housing authorities the Act describes those categories of homeless people who for the purposes of the Act have to be regarded as having priority need for accommodation. One of these is those who have accommodation but "cannot secure entry to it" or who would risk violence in occupying it (for example, battered women). Pregnant women also are specifically identified as having priority need.

There is no breakdown by sex of figures of those accepted by local authorities as homeless under the 1977 Act. However a comparison of the figures of homeless households accepted in the first half of 1978 and 1979 showed that over 80 per cent of the total of 26,460 and 27,620 respectively were groups in which women predominate.[29] These were households with dependent children or households where a member was pregnant or elderly.

Little research has been carried out on homeless women not in the priority categories of the 1977 Act or who have not applied for accommodation. It is known from the National Assistance Board report *Homeless Single Persons* (1966) and the O.P.C.S. report *Hostels and Lodgings for Single People* (1976) that women formed a smaller percentage than men.

The Act marked a step forward in clarifying responsibility for housing the homeless. Previously in a 1974 circular *Homelessness* local authorities had been asked to transfer the main responsibility for housing the homeless from social services to housing authorities. But by 1975 only two thirds had done this. In July 1976 a court ruled that the 1974 circular was not binding on local authorities. Later that year a Private Members Bill was introduced by Stephen Ross M.P. and this became the basis of the *Housing (Homeless Persons) Act 1977*.

The Joint Charities Group has been monitoring the implementation of this Act since it came into force in December 1977.[30] They reported that in the first four months, three of the duties laid down by the Act seem to have achieved significant improvements in the policies of housing authorities. These were: (a) the obligation not to split families when homeless, (b) the duty of councils to accept battered women with children as homeless, (c) the obligation to secure accommodation for those who are homeless or threatened with homelessness and in priority need. They went on, however, to discuss five aspects of the Act under which they considered that homeless households were receiving from local authorities either less protection than the government intended or discriminatory treatment.[31] These included defining people as 'intentionally homeless', and therefore not eligible under the Act, and not providing advice and appropriate assistance for non-priority need applicants. There was also concern about the standard of accommodation being offered to priority need applicants.

Lower income households

Lower income households were identified both in the D.O.E. *Housing Policy* Green Paper and by the Housing Corporation as disadvantaged groups so far as housing is concerned.

Again, a precise definition of this group is not easy, but in a recent article, 'The characteristics of low income households' in C.S.O. *Social Trends* No. 8 R. Van Slooten and A. G. Coverdale have attempted to give one. On the basis of net household income identified in the *Family Expenditure Survey* they took the bottom fifth (in terms of normal net household income) of people. What they found was that half the low income households were elderly. Single parent families were also very vulnerable. About half the pensioner and one parent households had low incomes.

It has already been shown that women predominate in both these groups, but there is additional evidence in the Van Slooten and Coverdale analysis. About half of both the male and female pensioners had low incomes. *Other* (i.e. non-pensioner) households were twice as likely to have a low income if they were headed by a woman.

For those who rent accommodation help can be sought from D.H.S.S. through supplementary benefits. There are also rent rebates (for local authority tenants) and rent allowances (for private and housing association tenants). For home owners on supplementary benefit help can be given with interest charges and for certain essential repairs (up to a specified sum which was £200 in 1979).

There has been much discussion about some of the problems connected with giving income related help[32] and there have been suggestions from many quarters that a universal housing benefit might be a fairer and more flexible way of giving help to everyone and not just those on supplementary benefit.

Others

Although women may not figure prominently in some of the other disadvantaged groups mentioned at the beginning of this chapter, particular sections within these groups do have their housing problems. For example although women do not predominate in ethnic minorities (numbers for the population from the New Commonwealth and Pakistan show more males in every age group except two, those for the 25–29 ages where there are more women and for the 30–34s where numbers are roughly equal) some do have housing problems. One group with problems may be women, such as nurses and hotel workers, whose accommodation is linked to a job. Particular stresses also seem to have arisen between parents of West Indian origin and their children brought up in England under a freer educational system. Such stresses may help bring about an increase in homelessness among young black people. Some specific projects have begun to help meet the needs of these groups. And married women from ethnic minority groups, particularly the Asian ones, may find it especially difficult to escape from a marriage which is unsatisfactory. The disapproval of marriage breakdown initiated by a woman may be so great that it is not possible to find accommodation within the ethnic community. Close relatives who might have offered support may not be available. Some Asian women have very little experience of 'negotiating' with the outside world and thus feel unable to cope with the situation. On the other hand Muslim Law allows easier divorce on religious grounds. The woman may feel a great deal of stigma and also be unused to coping on her own. Younger Asian women brought up in Britain are increasingly questioning traditional marriage arrangements, though many still remain contented with them.

Conclusions

This chapter began by identifying what it seems to be generally agreed are disadvantaged groups. Many of them, as has been seen, are predominantly female. The disadvantages they suffer from may be summed up as lack of access to suitable housing, lack of security and difficulties in becoming, and remaining, owner occupiers. Some of these problems stem from a lack of income, which restricts choice. But many advances have been made. The public sector (local authorities and housing associations) has paid far more attention to these groups and, in some cases, has discriminated positively in their favour (for example, the elderly and sheltered housing). The law has been changed in some respect to give women more rights. Voluntary bodies, in some cases self help groups (for example, women's aid groups), have sprung up in some areas to make greater provision. For almost every group mentioned it seems that housing conditions are beginning to improve. In the next chapter we examine some of the factors which have led to this improvement and sum up what still needs to be done.

References

1. M.H.L.G. *Council Housing Purposes, Procedures and Priorities* (the Cullingworth report), H.M.S.O., 1969.
2. D.O.E. *Housing Policy: A Consultative Document*, Cmnd. 6851, H.M.S.O., 1977.
3. The Housing Corporation, *The Selection of tenants by housing associations for subsidised schemes*, Circular 1/75, The Housing Corporation, 1975.
4. C.S.O. *Social Trends* No. 9, H.M.S.O., 1978, p. 62.
5. In a large survey of elderly people it was shown that 13.7 per cent of men suffered from rheumatism and arthritis compared with 23.1 per cent of women. A Hunt. *The Elderly at Home*, O.P.C.S., H.M.S.O., 1978, p. 71, Table 10.5.1. And in a survey of wheelchair users 2.7 per 1,000 of the female population and 1.8 per 1,000 of men in England and Wales came into this category. *Social Trends* No. 9, *op. cit.*, p. 72, Table 3.24.
6. D.H.S.S. *A Happier Old Age*, H.M.S.O., 1978, p. 9.
7. D.O.E. *National Dwelling and Housing Survey*, H.M.S.O., 1978, p. 35. For example 48.7 per cent of households in England where the head was over 65 lacked at least one basic amenity.
8. e.g. D.O.E. Design Bulletin 31, *Housing for the Elderly. The size of grouped schemes*, H.M.S.O., 1975, p. 24. 80 per cent of the sample were women.
   D. Boldy, P. Abel, and K. Carter. *The Elderly in Grouped Dwellings: A Profile*, University of Exeter, 1973, p. 11. 71 per cent of the sample were women.
   J. Attenburrow. *Grouped Housing for the elderly: a review of local authority provision and practice with particular reference to alarm systems*, D.O.E., Building Research Establishment, H.M.S.O., 1976. 78 per cent of the sample were women.
9. Boldy, *op. cit.*, p. 26, found that death accounted for 53 per cent of all movements out of sheltered housing in his sample of 1,220 tenants between 1963–71. Attenburrow, *op. cit.*, p. 20, found that 63 per cent of tenants who left the schemes in his sample were accounted for by death. Anchor Housing Association in *Caring for the Elderly in Sheltered Housing*, 1977, found in a survey of their tenants from 1973–76 that 484 (56 per cent) of the 866 tenants who had moved out had died.
10. These and subsequent figures are taken from A. Harris. *Handicapped and Impaired in Great Britain*, O.P.C.S., H.M.S.O., 1971.
11. C.S.O. *Social Trends* No. 9, *op. cit.*, p. 72.
12. S. Sainsbury. *Registered as Disabled*, George Bell and Sons, 1970.
13. J. Buckle. *Work and Housing of Impaired Persons in Great Britain*, H.M.S.O., 1971.
14. Central Council for the Disabled. Working Party on Housing, *Towards a Housing Policy for Disabled People*, Central Council for the Disabled, 1975, p. 6.
15. C.S.O. *Social Trends* No. 4, 'Mental illness and the psychiatric services' by E. R. Bransby, H.M.S.O., 1973.
16. D.H.S.S. *Better Services for the Mentally Handicapped*, Cmnd. 4683, H.M.S.O., 1971, p. 5.
17. D.H.S.S. *Better Services for the Mentally Ill*, Cmnd. 6233, H.M.S.O., 1975, p. 49.
18. By Cambridge City Council (see *Housing*, January, 1979, 'Housing the mentally ill and handicapped' by I. K. Mitchell pp. 5–7) and in South Cambridgeshire District Council (see *District Councils Review*, December 1975, 'Housing the mentally ill – a success story' by R. Page, pp. 314–16).

19. E. Durkin. *Hostels for the mentally disordered,* Young Fabian Pamphlet 24, Fabian Society, 1971.
20. R. Leete. 'One parent families: numbers and characteristics', *Population Trends* No. 13, H.M.S.O., Autumn, 1978.
21. D.O.E. *Housing Policy,* Technical Vol. 1, H.M.S.O., 1977, p. 114, Table 111.2.
22. D.H.S.S. *Report of the Committee on One-Parent Families* (the Finer report), Cmnd. 5629, Vol. 1. The Report, Vol. 2, Cmnd. 5629–1 Appendices, H.M.S.O., 1974.
23. R. Leete. *op. cit.*
24. E. Pizzey. *Scream quietly or the neighbours will hear,* Penguin, 1974, p. 142.
25. J. Pahl. *A Refuge for Battered Women,* H.M.S.O., 1978, p. 59.
26. D.O.E. *Housing Policy: A Consultative Document, op. cit.,* p. 112.
27. V. Binney, G. Harkell and J. Nixon. 'Refuge Provision for battered women', *Housing,* December, 1979, pp. 6–7.
28. J. Clegg. *Dictionary of Social Services,* Bedford Square Press, 1971, p. 41.
29. D.O.E. *Press Notice* 14.12.79.
30. Joint Charities Group. *The implementation of the Housing (Homeless Persons) Act 1977: An appraisal after four months,* April, 1978.
31. Some of these points are discussed by N. Raynsford, Director of S.H.A.C. in 'Homelessness', *Housing,* October, 1978, pp. 14–17.
32. D.O.E. *Housing Policy,* Technical Vol. 1, *op. cit.*

CHAPTER 4

How Change has been Achieved and What Remains to be Done

Introduction

The two previous chapters have shown some of the ways in which women are at a disadvantage in housing. It must be noted, however, that there have been considerable improvements for those in most of the groups described. For example, deserted and battered wives have been given greater security in relation to their homes, more women have become owner occupiers and there has been an increase in public provision for single parent mothers. There have also been important changes in the law, in the practice of the administering organisations and in general attitudes, all of which are closely and necessarily linked.

But not all the difficulties have yet been overcome, so it is worthwhile analysing how the changes that have been made have come about. This analysis may give a clue as to how the changes that are still needed can be achieved.

The reasons for change

It is only rarely that changes in social policy take place as a result of one cause. It is more usual for there to be a combination of events or for changes to evolve by slow process (incremental change).

What were the factors that have had the most impact on the position of women and their housing rights? Common to all the changes described in earlier chapters has been the importance of people's *attitudes*. Changes in the law or in practice would have been much more difficult had it not been for the changes taking place in social attitudes. This was the single most important reason for such improvements in women's access to housing as have been achieved. However, much still remains to be done, and the relation of changing attitudes to future action is discussed in the last chapter.

Other important instruments of change are research, the influence of individuals, pressure groups and the media, the women's movement and the Equal Opportunities Commission together with women's greater financial independence.

Research, individuals, pressure groups and the media

Research has played an important part in identifying problems. The Finer report on *One-Parent Families* with its careful analysis of the housing and the other conditions of single parent families has made it difficult for policy makers to ignore either the scale or the extent of the needs of this group.[1]

Research on the elderly such as that done by Peter Townsend in *The Last Refuge* (1962) and Amelia Harris, notably in the Government Social Survey report *Social Welfare for the Elderly* in 1968, helped to change the emphasis from residential care to keeping people in their own homes. Research sponsored by the Equal Opportunities Commission on the discrimination women face in getting a mortgage is likely to make it less easy for building societies to treat women differently from men.

Research, however, can only provide the evidence and point in a particular direction. It cannot of itself change policy, but it can be used as a weapon by those who wish to make changes.

Individuals too have always had a key role in achieving changes in social policy. Some of the most notable have been women. From Florence Nightingale to Erin Pizzey there have always been women who have helped to shape policy. Sometimes this has been by identifying a gap in provision and then setting about attempting to fill it, as Erin Pizzey has done with refuges for battered women. Sometimes the influence an individual woman has had has been at a national policy level. For example, it was a woman M.P., Jo Richardson, who sponsored the *Domestic Violence and Matrimonial Proceedings Act 1976* as a private Members Bill.

Pressure groups have also played their part in this as in other fields. Writing about social change in Britain 1970–75 in *Social Trends* the Central Statistical Office commented "Many minority groups became more vocal than before, and the role of pressure groups for minorities was increasingly accepted by both public and government."[2] A great many of the groups have centred round particular disadvantaged groups such as those for single parent families and single women with dependants. But others have taken a more general interest. For example, the National Federation of Women's Institutes and the National Union of Townswomen's Guilds have given evidence to committees such as the Parker Morris one on housing standards. It will be interesting to see whether the more broadly based groups now springing up, such as Women in Architecture, the New Architecture Movement Feminist Group and Women in Housing, will have more effect.

It is always difficult to assess the influence of the media. Programmes such as 'Cathy Come Home' or 'I don't want to be a burden' produced no immediate changes in policy towards the homeless or the elderly. However, the longer term effect is likely to be more subtle through the influence on people's attitudes. In the same way programmes that reinforce traditional stereotypes may have a negative effect by delaying change.

Women's greater financial independence, the women's movement and the Equal Opportunities Commission

An important cause of change has been women's greater financial independence which has given some women a greater range of choice.

Although, on average, women still earn considerably less than men, there are many jobs such as those in teaching, the civil service and local government where there has been equality of salaries for many years. And the growth in the number of married women in paid employment has increased their independence by giving them an income which is separate from that of their husbands. The ability to exercise choice in housing is to a great extent related to income. Other changes, including improved methods of birth control, can give women more choice over the number of children they have and over their timing so that they may, if they wish, return to work. But for some vulnerable groups, of course, such as battered wives and the homeless, that choice will probably have been made before their housing problem becomes acute.

It is very difficult to link changes of policy directly to action by the women's movement. But there is certainly some connection both in regard to changes in policy of housing agencies and to changes in direct provision. For example, the National Women's Aid Federation claims to have brought about both. Jo Richardson, M.P., acknowledges that without the help she received from the N.W.A.F. and others her *Domestic Violence and Matrimonial Proceedings Act 1976* would probably have foundered.[3] In this way they contributed to a change in the law, but at the same time they have also, through their local branches, provided refuges for battered women.

It is probably too early to assess the influence of the Equal Opportunities Commission. Reference has already been made to their sponsorship of research on mortgages. They have the duty to investigate and to serve discrimination notices and so could be a powerful agent of change in relation to the housing rights of women. Some have criticised their lack of activity but it may be that it is the legislation which is weak.

What is needed – introduction

The most fundamental change that is needed is a change in attitudes so this forms the basis of the conclusions. (See Chapter 11.) But other changes are also required. First, there are some changes which would enable women to gain easier access to each type of tenure and give them greater security and better conditions there. Then there are changes related to the provision of accommodation. Finally, some new approaches are considered.

What is needed – easier access, greater rights, and better conditions in each tenure

Those concerned with groups in special need are agreed on the importance of the groups having equal access to the different forms of housing tenure and also to the same quality of accommodation as others. One view is that it must be made "easier for people to obtain the tenure they want. More and more people would like to become home owners, or to enter the newer forms of tenure combining some of the advantages of home ownership and renting,"[4] Disadvantaged groups would be helped to become home owners by the availability of more favourable loans or grants to first time buyers and by an extension of lending on older property by building societies, especially in urban areas. The right to buy council homes will also help those women who are already in council accommodation, but it has been pointed out that other disadvantaged women who are living in flats (such as single parent families) may become worse off, if fewer council houses become available for them to move to. The difficulties of low income owner occupiers should not, however, be ignored.

There are many groups who may want to move to other tenures. Battered women may, for example, want to move from a refuge to council accommodation or need help to become owner occupiers. Elderly women are another group who may wish to change tenure. They may wish to rent when they can no longer cope with their own home. Or they may occupy tied accommodation and find that when they retire they have nowhere to live. Or they may want, or have to move from, accommodation in the private rented sector. Of the 18,000 widowed or divorced women accepted for council accommodation in 1973 in England and Wales 12,000 are estimated to have come from the privately rented sector and about half the rest were previously owner occupiers.[5] To get into each tenure it is necessary to fulfil certain criteria, such as having enough money for a deposit, being able to comply with the conditions for a council tenancy, or being acceptable to a private landlord. The measures mentioned earlier to make it easier to become an owner occupier and to ease restrictions on entry to a council list would all help. Other measures would help women to change tenure. For example local authorities have the power to buy a separated wife's home and then grant her a new mortgage (or part mortgage) thus enabling her to remain where she is. Or they may accept her as a council tenant if she so prefers. It would be helpful if measures like this could be more widely publicised.

Access to the local authority sector may be crucial for women who, as was seen in Chapter 2, are more likely to rent. The figures are particularly striking for divorced and separated women where local authorities play a major part in the provision of housing. There is also evidence that in some of the disadvantaged households mentioned earlier where women predominate a similar pattern can be found. Single parent families are one group. Low income households, many of whom will be single persons, also look to the council sector. About half of all low income households in the United Kingdom were council tenants in 1975 compared with one third of other households.[6]

Those who look to the public sector for their housing needs want policies which do not exclude them automatically on certain counts. In 1969 the Cullingworth Committee recommended that there should be no residential qualification for admission to a housing list. They considered that "no one should be precluded from applying for, or being considered for, a council tenancy on any ground whatsoever".[7] More recently there has been a fair measure of agreement that what is required is maximum freedom (not necessarily a statutory framework) for local authorities while at the same time an end to the practice of imposing residential or other qualifications for inclusion on a housing list. Not insisting on a residential qualification may also help groups such as the mentally ill who have been in hospital for a long time and have lost their home links. D.H.S.S. in their White Paper in 1975 *Better Services for the Mentally Ill* made the point that some hospital patients may no longer have contact with the place from which they originally came, but may well have developed a number of links in the area of the hospital. It was hoped that in such cases local authorities would be able to make it possible for them to make a home in the neighbourhood of the hospital.

But women who gain equal right of access to council housing lists may still be disadvantaged, for example, by a heavily weighted allocation of points for length of residence in an area. The Finer committee on *One-Parent Families* urged that, after admission to the waiting list, claims should be considered solely by reference to an assessment of need. The same argument applied to other groups beside one-parent families.

The achievement of a place on a housing list (or register) and then ultimately of being offered council accommodation is not necessarily sufficient in itself. Some groups are maintaining that the accommodation actually offered can be inferior to that offered to other groups. The Housing Services Advisory Group claimed that "there is ample evidence that discrimination against lone parents in the quality of house and area they receive is the rule rather than the exception. Single mothers are treated the worst but all fatherless families tend to be to some extent stigmatised and hence given the most stigmatised lettings".[8]

Another example of a group who may only be offered a particular type of accommodation is the elderly. Old people who are owner occupiers or who move from another area may find themselves ineligible for ordinary council accommodation but accepted for sheltered housing. They may accept this even though all they really want is small easy-to-run accommodation.

We take up the case for more positive discrimination later in this chapter.

Housing associations offer particular advantages in that they may be able to cater for special needs in a way that local authorities do not find themselves able to do. They may, for example, be able to house owner occupiers or those lacking a residential qualification. In some cases the local authority has a nomination agreement with the housing association and may itself nominate people to categories it normally excludes and whose need may be 'suppressed'. Housing associations increasingly give priority to special groups into which many women fall. Hence a good deal of new provision is for these groups and in particular the elderly and disabled. This provision is in line with the advice given in the Cohen report *Housing Associations* (1971) which said that housing associations were especially well placed to help certain groups with special housing needs. Local authorities may recognise these needs but may not always be able to give them priority over 'general family' provision.[9] The importance of the role of housing associations was underlined in a White Paper *Widening The Choice: The Next Steps in Housing* in 1973. In a nutshell what housing associations should aim for, said the Housing Corporation who fund many schemes is "an alternative to, as well as a complement of, local authority renting".[10] It is interesting that a few housing associations have been exclusively for women (for example the Women's Pioneer Housing Association which was established in 1920 to provide housing for single working women in London).

There are also arguments in favour of greater security of tenure for, despite changes in the law, some women do face problems of uncertainty about retaining an existing home. If they are in a home owned by their husband they may shrink from a court case to establish their right to remain. If they are renting, practice seems to vary over whether the tenancy is automatically transferred to the woman. If there are children, this is more likely but what of the couple without children who split up? It is difficult to argue that each should have an automatic right to a tenancy. But at least the woman should have as much right as the man even if the rent book is in his name.

Another group who face similar problems over security are single women caring for elderly relatives. The National Council for the Single Woman and her Dependants have argued that where an adult child has lived in the family home and cared for an aged or infirm parent, she should have the right to continued occupation of the home for life after the second parent has died. They say that "as the law now stands the family home will on intestacy have to be sold for the benefit of the surviving children, and this can work very harshly where there is only one who has stayed at home to look after the old parents".[11]

Housing association tenants have been in the same position as those in local authority accommodation in having had no statutory security of tenure. However, as with local authorities tenancies, this will be changed under the *Housing Bill 1980*. One disadvantage for housing association tenants is that rents, as set by the rent officer, are sometimes higher than for a local authority tenancy.

In the private sector women may find it difficult to gain access to rented accommodation but, where they have, they are likely to have enjoyed statutory security of tenure. However, their housing conditions are likely to be less good than those of people in other tenures.

As far as conditions are concerned we concentrate on those who rent either from local authorities or housing associations. This is partly because some of the features related to owner occupation have already been mentioned (for example, better knowledge about the right to remain in the marital home) and partly because conditions can be controlled to a greater extent by an owner than by a tenant. Renting, from whatever the agency, gives freedom in certain respects such as limited or no responsibility for repairs and the avoidance of problems over buying and selling. Many women welcome this. However, the advantages are counteracted by other factors such as constraints on what is done to the property and the payment of money for something which may never (or is unlikely) to be owned.

Local authority tenants are more likely to enjoy better housing conditions than many, though not all, other groups. For example, of the six tenure groups identified in the D.O.E. *National Dwelling and Housing Survey* (1978) those in local authority property were more likely than any group, except those owning with a mortgage or loan, to have sole use of all the basic amenities. But against this has to be balanced the lack of freedom local authority tenants have to modernise, decorate and alter their property. The tenants' charter which forms part of the *Housing Bill 1980* should give tenants in local authority accommodation more freedom in such matters.

In housing management the move towards greater tenant participation could allow women to communicate their views and hopefully influence policy in local authorities. Many tenant groups have women among their leading members. In a measured summary of various tenant schemes Ann Richardson concluded that, while not a panacea, they "can prove useful devices for helping to ensure greater attention to tenants problems".[12]

What is needed – changes in provision and practice

More of existing forms of provision

It seems generally agreed that one of the greatest needs is for more small homes. As the 1975 D.O.E. Circular (74/75): *Housing: Needs and Action* put it "More than half the households in Britain now consist of only one or two people. These small households include people of all ages in a wide range of domestic circumstances."[13] Some of these households such as single parent families and the elderly will be predominantly women.

In 1975 the D.O.E. study *The Need for Smaller Homes* concluded that the need for smaller homes was likely to increase and that not all the groups in need would have their needs met by existing homes.[14] A 1980 D.O.E. report *Starter Homes* gave details of one and two bedroom starter and extendible homes for sale.[15] While most of the buyers were young couples there were also some elderly people and separated and divorced people starting out on their own. It was the low price rather than the size which seemed to attract buyers. In another study *The Mobile Homes Review* which was based on a survey in 1975 it was noted that the residents were different from those in 1959.[16] Previously, the great majority were young or youngish married couples. But in 1977 there were proportionately more young, elderly and small households than in the population as a whole and incomes in all age groups were generally below the national average. The characteristics described mean that many of the occupants were likely to be women. The committee concluded that despite the financial and legal disadvantages, mobile homes were clearly popular with those who lived in them and should continue to play a role in meeting housing needs, albeit a small one.

Apart from small homes a more intensive use of existing accommodation might help. Being able to become a lodger helps those who do not want, or are not able, to obtain self-contained accommodation. Similarly multi-occupation of housing, while not usually looked on very favourably, can answer particular needs and sharing may be acceptable to certain groups, "either because they wish to minimise their housing costs, or because their demands on their accommodation are small or because some form of communal life suits their needs".[17] A speaker at a Rights of Women Workshop on housing in 1978 claimed that sharing a house might be a better arrangement for two single parent families and preferable to their occupying two small flats. Sharing, in certain circumstances, helps to increase the supply of accommodation for small households, and it was encouraged as a matter of policy in the D.O.E. circular *Better use of vacant and underoccupied housing* in 1977 provided adequate amenities were provided and the property was properly managed. Experiments in communal living or sharing have been going on for many years. In the 1960s and 1970s they were often linked with the 'ecology' movement. However they had little impact on housing design, and if people want to buy suitable old housing for this purpose more financial institutions must be willing to lend to this kind of buyer.

Another example of a form of provision which might be extended is 'boarding out' or fostering which up to now has long been used for children. This may be a helpful form of housing for some groups of women, such as the mentally ill or the elderly.

Special types of accommodation

It is generally agreed that only a minority of people need specially designed or adapted housing. For example some elderly people need the sort of small, easy-to-run homes with the support of close neighbours and a warden which can be found in sheltered housing. Very young single mothers who have never run a home of their own may benefit from grouped living with some support and this is what some may want. Some severely handicapped people need wheelchair housing. It is worth noting that one of these groups is entirely female and that women form the majority in the other two.

Other women may want some special form of accommodation temporarily. A hostel may be helpful for some mentally disordered people until they find their feet and can move into homes of their own. The same is true for some battered women.

How many specialised units are needed is a matter for argument. The D.O.E. tend not to lay down norms for types of provision preferring to leave it to the discretion of individual local authorities. Some groups and individuals argue for places related to population. For example the National Women's Aid Federation in their leaflet *Heads they win, tails we lose* claim that there should be one family place in a refuge for every 10,000 population. Nicholas Bosanquet and others have pleaded that standards should be laid down for so many sheltered housing places per elderly population.[18]

Some types of housing which are special, such as bed and breakfast accommodation for the homeless, may be highly unsatisfactory.

Easier exchanges and transfers

Some women wish to move from one area to another. This may be quite a short distance within the local authority area, or it may mean crossing a boundary from one local authority to another.

The reason why they want to move may be to get away from some situation such as being battered or, simply, to be nearer to their relatives either to be helped by them or to give support to them. Evidence is given in Anthea

Tinker's *Housing the Elderly near Relatives* that there are not inconsiderable numbers of the elderly who want to move closer to relatives.[19]

While it is understandable that authorities like to give preference to their own residents, flexible policies to allow people to move more easily would be helpful to many women. They would also encourage some groups, such as those elderly who are underoccupying, to move to something smaller and more convenient, thus releasing a needed family house. If it is not possible for people to arrange mutual exchanges, it would be helpful if discretion were given to housing staff to accept people in need. The case for the abolition of residential qualifications has already been put. It is fortunate that housing associations are sometimes able to take groups who are not necessarily eligible for local authority housing.

More advice for women

Most housing research concerned with women comes out in favour of more advice. Unless women are aware of the options there is the danger that they will take the wrong decisions such as giving up their home without being aware of their rights. Jo Tunnard in a paper *Women and Housing: owner occupation* prepared for a Shelter Conference expressed the view that ignorance was one of the major factors preventing single parents from keeping their homes, or making it impossible for them to buy another. The options on types of tenure may need explaining. Legal rights may need spelling out. In some cases it may be very practical advice that is required, such as that given by occupational therapists to the disabled about adaptations needed in the home.

One of the three main recommendations of the Shelter Housing Aid Centre, based on the evidence of need presented by women coming to them and on a survey of London Boroughs, was with regard to the availability of aid and advice. In *Violence in Marriage* (1976) they suggested that women subject to, or threatened with, violence needed access to a Primary Advisory Service – whether an advisor or a team of advisors. Many local authorities and some voluntary bodies do now run housing aid or advice centres and this service has expanded rapidly in the last ten years.

All who come into contact with women who have housing problems need to be trained if they are to give accurate advice. Professionals, particularly social workers, and volunteers including those who man Citizens Advice Bureaux, all need up-to-date information about the law, council procedures and the availability of different kinds of housing. Some solicitors for instance, may not be familiar with the mechanics of a mortgage and how it is possible to keep this going while on supplementary benefit. There is particular need to ensure that staff in housing departments are adequately trained and are aware of what Mary Smith has called "the objectives and constraints of other services".[20] This is especially necessary where the law is complex as it is over single parent families.

Many other suggestions have been made that might improve the advice given to women about housing. Jo Tunnard has made a number of recommendations with regard to the practice of building societies. These include the suggestion that they should always invite a borrower whose account is in arrears to come and discuss the matter with them instead of issuing a standard letter with a threat of legal action.[21] Another idea she puts forward is that building societies should prepare a leaflet which sets out the ways in which a deserted wife can reduce the outgoings on the marital home, clear any arrears on the mortgage, and make provision for future payments.

Another useful way of disseminating advice is the short easy-to-read pamphlet. Good examples are D.O.E.'s *One-Parent Families: A Guide to Housing Aid* (1978) and S.H.A.C.'s *A Woman's Place* (1979) by Maureen Leevers and Pat Thynne.

Closer links between departments and agencies

There are many instances where women would benefit from closer links between departments, particularly between housing and social services. They would gain too from more contact between the local authority and voluntary bodies such as the National Women's Aid Federation.

The Morris Committee was particularly concerned about links between housing and social services.[22] Although their report, *Housing and Social Work: a joint approach,* related to Scotland, it provided useful evidence about where co-operation is crucial. They highlighted the lack of understanding that departments had about their respective roles, the importance of joint involvement in the allocation and transfer of council tenancies and the need for social work support for tenants with problems. They also stressed the need for a joint strategy so that services for vulnerable groups are planned coherently.

Apart from the obvious advantages of joint co-ordinating machinery (which may be easier if the two departments are part of the same authority) there are other things that would help. Joint training and/or placements of staff could increase knowledge and understanding, and joint research in matters of common concern, such as elderly homeless women, might contribute to giving a better service. There is need too for co-ordination with bodies such as the Supplementary Benefits Commission. In special cases (for example where a woman is subject to violence) there may be need to bring in other groups such as the police.

The value of statutory bodies having close links with voluntary organisations has been underlined by a number of reports such as that of the Wolfenden committee.[23] In the London Borough of Haringey one suggestion put by the Borough Housing Officer was that the housing service should nominate one officer to be responsible for all liaison with their local women's aid group and that all possible steps should be taken to improve the level of support given to this group.

The closer the housing service comes to being a 'comprehensive' service, that is looking at the total needs and resources of an area rather than just the council sector, the more likely it is to be able to help those women who are in vulnerable groups or in situations outside the council net. A summary of suggested responsibilities was given by the D.O.E. Housing Services Advisory Group in *Organising a Comprehensive Housing Service* in 1978.

New approaches

Positive discrimination?

A more controversial way of change is that of positive discrimination (now often called affirmative policies), that is giving extra help to disadvantaged groups. The advantage of such a policy is that it concentrates help on those who really need it. A disadvantage is that other groups lose out. For example, a positive policy of discrimination towards one-parent families could be held to be unfair to two parent families.

There is already some discrimination in housing policies. Most points schemes have some elements of favouring one group rather than another. They are, as the Cullingworth committee put it "an attempt to weigh the relative claims of applicants in greatly different circumstances. They are excellent in concept but exceedingly difficult to devise in detail with fairness".[24] Even more difficult are 'merit' schemes where there is said to be more freedom for the exercise of judgement.

The view expressed in the *Housing Policy* Green Paper was that it was quite clear that some discrimination was needed and not just in the public rented sector. It was held that a reasonable degree of priority in access to public rented sector housing and home ownership was needed for people in housing need who in the past had found themselves at the end of the queue.

Another way of giving extra priority to disadvantaged groups is to draw up special schemes to help with payment of some of the costs of housing. Rent rebates, rate rebates and housing allowances are all examples. But the problems, such as the low level of take-up, are well known and in housing those in the private rented sector, where many women are housed, have a lower take-up rate than those in the public sector.

The question arises whether a more forceful policy of positive discrimination is called for. In the United States a separate department was set up in 1976 called the Women's Policy and Program Division in the Department of Housing and Urban Development. Describing the work of her department, the Director stated two of the aims. These were developing and funding projects addressed particularly to women's needs, such as crisis centres for battered wives, and the encouragement of women's groups to take on the monitoring of H.U.D.'s programmes to widen a woman's choice of housing.[25] It seems doubtful whether an interventionist role of this sort would be acceptable in this country unless public opinion was firmly behind it.

New types of tenure and provison?

While many women are concerned simply about getting equal access to ordinary housing, it is possible that some of the newer kinds of tenure and provision may offer positive advantages. Equity sharing (part rent, part mortgage such as that pioneered by the City of Birmingham) is one possibility of a new type of tenure. Co-ownerhsip and housing co-operatives are also possibilities which may be suited to women. An example of one co-operative, formed by women for women, is Seagull Housing Co-operative which started by obtaining a house from the Notting Hill Housing Trust. In a leaflet members described how they started. "Most of us have been living in squats or short-life accommodation. However, with the ending of squatting as a viable possibility we were forced to find ways of obtaining permanent housing for ourselves. Being single and of low to middle income (as women generally are) the usual methods of council waiting lists and building society mortgages were out of our reach. We had heard about housing co-ops and decided to investigate the possibility of forming a women's co-op."

There may also be some scope for developing alternative forms of tenure in the private sector, such as some of the Leasehold Retirement schemes being set up for the elderly. Some of the latter are in a sense hybrid schemes because they may have an element of subsidy in the capital cost.

Changes in the law

Although recent changes in the law have given women more rights and greater protection there are further improvements which would help. Some, such as the right to buy, greater security in the public sector and a tenants charter are contained in the *Housing Bill 1980*.

Two groups who might particularly benefit from changes are women who have been assaulted and cohabitees. Anna Coote and Tess Gill in *Battered Women and the New Law* suggest that the *Domestic Violence and Matrimonial Proceedings Act 1976* should be extended to apply to violence inflicted by other members of the family (for example by a son on his mother). They also suggest that the protection offered to married women under the *Domestic Proceedings and Magistrates Act 1978* should be extended to cohabitees. Other suggestions they make are that there should be greater consistency between judges and that a system of Family Courts would be advantageous.

Conclusions

It is not enough to identify a problem for change to be achieved. George and Wilding have argued that four things are necessary before a social problem even gets to this stage.[26] They say it must be visible and measurable, it must challenge society's values, it must pose problems for all society and not just that group, and the condition has to be one which can be changed or is capable of improvement. But they insist that, even where these conditions are fulfilled, there may still be reasons why the recognition of a social problem does not lead to social action. Reasons why action does not always take place include the opinion that it is not an issue in which government should intervene, that the time is not ripe, that there are insufficient resources and the feeling that action would contravene society's social values.

In the case of women all these reasons have been put forward and they are discussed further in the last chapter. Whether women will now sit back and accept them is another matter. For although the position of women as consumers has improved there are still further advances that could be made. More consultation about design, more attention to the single, more help for first time purchasers, measures to give better accommodation and greater security to groups of vulnerable women such as the single, the battered and the homeless are all needed. Much will depend on those who provide and take the decisions about housing and it is with this that the next part of the book is concerned.

References

1. D.H.S.S. *Report of the Committee on One-Parent Families,* (the Finer report), Cmnd. 5629, H.M.S.O., 1974.
2. C.S.O. *Social Trends* No. 7, H.M.S.O., 1976. p. 9.
3. A. Coote and T. Gill. *Battered Women and the New Law,* Interaction Imprint and National Council for Civil Liberties, 1977, p. 3. (Revised and reprinted 1979.)
4. D.O.E. *Housing Policy: A Consultative Document,* Cmnd. 6851, H.M.S.O., 1977, p. 8.
5. D.O.E. *Housing Policy:* Technical Volume Part III, H.M.S.O., 1977, p. 13.
6. C.S.O. *Social Trends* No. 8, H.M.S.O., 1977, p. 35.
7. M.H.L.G. *Council Housing Purposes, Procedures and Priorities* (the Cullingworth report), H.M.S.O., 1969, p. 54.
8. D.O.E. Housing Services Advisory Group, *The Housing of One-Parent Families,* D.O.E. 1978, p. 8.
9. D.O.E. Central Housing Advisory Committee, *Housing Associations,* (the Cohen report), H.M.S.O., 1971, p. 8.
10. The Housing Corporation. *The Selection of tenants by housing associations for subsidised schemes,* Circular 1/75, The Housing Corporation, 1975, p. 1.
11. R. Arnold. 'The inequitable treatment for those caring for elderly or infirm relatives', *Poverty,* No. 28, Spring, 1974.
12. A. Richardson. *Tenant participation in council housing management,* D.O.E., Housing Development Directorate, Occasional Paper 2/77, H.M.S.O., 1977, chap. 11.
13. D.O.E. *Housing: Needs and Action,* Circular 74/75, H.M.S.O., 1975, para. 6.
14. R. Mainwaring and E. Young. *The need for smaller homes,* D.O.E., Housing Development Directorate, 1975.
15. R. Mainwaring and E. Young. *Starter Homes,* D.O.E., Housing Development Directorate, Occasional Paper 2/80, H.M.S.O., 1980.
16. D.O.E. and W. O. *Report of the Mobile Homes Review,* H.M.S.O., 1977.
17. M. Brion. 'Is there a future for multi-occupation?', *Housing Review,* July/August, 1974.
18. N. Bosanquet. *A Future for Old Age,* Temple Smith and New Society, 1978. pp. 102–3.
19. A. Tinker. *Housing the Elderly near Relatives: Moving and Other Options,* D.O.E., Housing Development Directorate, Occasional Paper 1/80, H.M.S.O., 1980.
20. M. E. H. Smith. *Guide to Housing,* Housing Centre Trust, 1977, p. 351.
21. J. Tunnard. *No Father, No Home?,* C.P.A.G., 1976.
22. Scottish Development Department. *Housing and Social Work: a joint approach* (the Morris report), H.M.S.O., 1075.
23. Lord Wolfenden. *The Future of Voluntary Organisations* (the Wolfenden report), Croom Helm, 1978, chap. 5.
24. Cullingworth report, *op. cit.,* p. 42.
25. A. J. Skinner. 'Women Consumers, Women Professionals', National Association of Housing and Redevelopment Officials, *Journal of Housing,* U.S.A., Vol. 35, No. 5, May 1978.
26. V. George and P. Wilding. *Motherless Families,* Routledge and Kegan Paul, 1972, chap. 7.

CHAPTER 5

The General Picture

Introduction

The second part of this book is concerned with women in the housing service. What sort of jobs do they do? Are women in housing more or less likely to get to the top than in other jobs? Has the situation changed since the first entry of women into this type of work and, if so, how?

In talking about the housing service we include the public bodies concerned with the provision of housing – central government departments, local authorities and the housing associations. A good description of the roles of these organisations for those unfamiliar with them is given in Mary Smith's *Guide to Housing* (1977). There is little information available specifically about the employment of women in housing. We have been able to use small amounts of nationally published data but our main source of information has been the national survey and the *Housing Staff* survey carried out by the Education and Training for Housing Work Project at The City University in 1976–77 and described in the Appendix. These surveys provide us with a snapshot of the position of women in housing organisations although they were not specifically designed for this. The deficiencies of these data sources are discussed in the Appendix.

The national data and the *Housing Staff* study showed that few women held positions of influence in housing. This seems strange when we consider that women were regarded as the pioneers of housing management. We therefore look back at some of the early pioneers and, in the following three chapters, trace their careers and influence. In particular we look at the rise and fall of their own professional association. But to begin with we will survey the general scene as it was in 1976–78, first of all in central government and then in the local authorities and housing associations.

Women employed in housing organisations

Central government

In the civil service there have been few women at the top in the Department of the Environment, or its predecessor the Ministry of Housing and Local Government. One notable exception in the past was Dame Evelyn Sharp who was the Permanent Secretary at the Ministry of Housing and Local

Government from 1955 to 1966. But in 1978 of the posts at the level of Under-Secretary or above the only woman was the head of the Housing Development Directorate (an architect). In *The Civil Service Year Book 1978* under the Department of the Environment – Housing there were listed 16 Administrative jobs, four Under-Secretaries (all men), nine Assistant Secretaries (all men): the Director of Housing Development (a woman) and two Assistant Directors of Housing Development (both men). The Principal Planner in the Social Research Division was a woman. The significance of jobs at Assistant Secretary level can be illustrated by the fact that these are the staff who sign circulars. The head of the Housing Services Advisory Unit was a man but subsequently one man and one woman were appointed as Housing Services Advisers.

This picture is very similar to the rest of the civil service. Figures produced by the Civil Service Department for administrative staff in 1978 show that overall only 3 per cent of Under-Secretaries and above were women and 5 per cent of Assistant Secretaries were women. On the other hand 63 per cent of clerical officers and 79 per cent of clerical assistants (the lowest grade) were women. The number of women employed, except at clerical levels, is small. Nor has there been much change since 1950 except that the proportion of clerical grade staff who were women rose dramatically from 48 per cent in 1950 to 70 per cent in 1978.

Local government and housing associations

Local authorities and housing associations are the agencies concerned with the provision of public and social housing and it is with them that the remainder of this chapter is concerned. In 1976 about 34,500 non manual staff worked in local authority housing departments or sections.[1] A further 12,000 staff worked for housing associations but this figure included manual staff and a much larger proportion of part time staff.

In common with the civil service the general grade pattern for housing organisations is to have a large proportion of staff on lower grades. The proportion of staff on Senior Officer (S.O.) grades and above was less than 12 per cent. (Local authority grades were used for this analysis with housing association staff being given their nearest equivalent.) The *Housing Staff* sample was stratified to include adequate representation of higher grades. Figure 5.1 shows how the men and women in the sample were distributed within each grade. It graphically illustrates the lowly position of women within housing organisations. For example, of the 124 staff in the sample at Principal Officer (P.O.) level and above, 91 per cent were men and 9 per cent were women. Conversely, of the 213 clerical grade staff 22 per cent were men and 78 per cent were women. The middle level Administrative and Professional (A.P.) grades were more evenly distributed but with men still predominating in the higher grades (A.P. 4–5 grades have more responsibility than 1–3 and higher pay.) Overall the distribution was neatly asymmetrical with men in the overwhelming preponderance at the top grades and women at the bottom.

Thus the structures of housing organisations show a striking difference

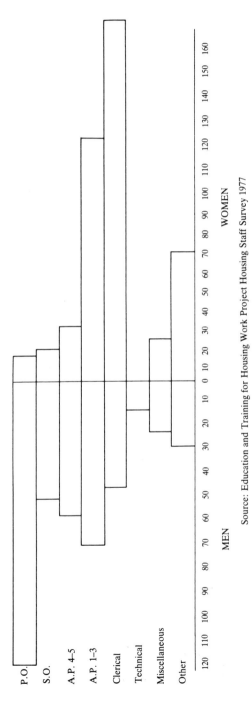

Figure 5.1
Distribution by grade of men and women in the staff study sample

Source: Education and Training for Housing Work Project Housing Staff Survey 1977

between the grades of men and women. In the following sections we look in a little more detail at the kinds of work commonly done by men and women in housing. All the information, apart from that on Chief Officers comes from the *Housing Staff* study which defined jobs in terms of levels of responsibility as well as grade.

Differences in the kind of work done by men and women
Chief Officers

In 1976 only 14 out of 403 local authorities had a woman as Chief Officer of a housing department and in 1977 the number had only increased by one (Table 5.1). This table shows that London Boroughs were marginally more likely to employ a woman than District Councils. However in related jobs (Table 5.2) the position was even worse. There was no woman as Chief Architect in a local authority in either 1976 or 1977. A report by the Royal Institute of British Architects commented, "Women are under-represented in the higher paid, more responsible positions."[2] In 1976 and 1977 there were two Chief Planning Officers (0.5 per cent) who were women. Both were employed by County Councils. A glance at the other Chief Officer posts (Table 5.2) shows that there is an abysmal lack of women in other departments. Social Services head the list with nine per cent and Housing comes second with four per cent. Trailing behind come Chief Education Officers (two per cent) and Chief Executives (0.2 per cent).

Table 5.1

Women chief officers in housing departments: England and Wales

	1976		1977	
	Nos.	%	Nos.	%
London	3	9	3	9
District Councils	11	3	12	4
Total	14	4	15	4

Source: *Municipal Year Books*, 1977 and 1978.

Table 5.2

Women chief officers in local authorities: England and Wales

	1976		1977	
	Nos.	%	Nos.	%
Directors of Social Services	10	7	10	9
Directors of Housing/Chief Housing Officers	14	4	15	4
Chief Education Officers	2	2	2	2
Planning Officers	2	0.5	2	0.5
Chief Executives	1	0.2	1	0.2
Chief Architects	0	0	0	0

Source: *Municipal Year Books*, 1977 and 1978.

In fact, as Sir Alan Dawtry, President of the Society of Local Authority Chief Officers, pointed out, in terms of actual numbers there were more women Chief Officers in housing than in any other service (15 as opposed to 10 Directors of Social Services).[3] But because there were nearly four times as many housing authorities as social services authorities the proportion works out as less.

Section heads

Below staff in upper management are staff described in the City University survey as 'section heads'. They were defined as being responsible for the supervision of a group of staff carrying out a particular function or functions. A section could be as small as two staff or as big as 20 but would often be in the range of 6–12 staff.

Out of the 173 section heads 23 per cent were women. This overall figure again concealed a number of variations. The first difference was between departments and associations. Out of their 68 section heads, associations had 35 per cent women and 65 per cent men. On the other hand in departments there were 105 section heads in the sample but only 15 per cent were women. This indication that for some reason or other women are much more likely to reach at least the first rung of senior jobs in associations than they are in housing departments must be treated with caution. First of all the sample of section heads was relatively small and secondly the difficulties in defining the level of jobs across organisations of different types must be kept in mind. Nevertheless the deduction that women may be somewhat better off in housing associations receives some support later in this study.

The second set of differences between section heads was in the housing functions in which they were employed. Of the 40 women section heads 29 (73 per cent) were in 'Management' (i.e. estate management). Three were in charge of development, technical or rehabilitation work and eight were in 'Administration or Finance'. Again only two of this eight were in departments, six were in associations. Although these numbers are small they are of some interest as it can be argued that in associations finance is more complicated than in housing departments where the accounts are usually passed to the treasurer at an intermediate stage.

It is usually on staff at this level that the job of answering non routine correspondence, particularly councillors' or M.P.s' queries, falls. People who cannot get the housing they want, not surprisingly, feel very strongly about it. Sometimes they feel that housing staff are unsympathetic. It is usually the section head or his deputy who is called in to help when situations threaten to become out of hand. Thus section heads are often in very stressful jobs at the point of conflict between the demands of the public, lower level staff and senior management. Not surprisingly they suffer some frustration, "Can't delegate because of staff quality – low grades mean low quality staff" is not an uncommon complaint. For many, though, the demands of the job are part of its satisfactions – the woman who "found the job very frustrating at first because there was no system of records, and bad contractors were being used, but now enjoys the challenge and feels that things are improving daily", and the man who is "basically very happy in his work: likes the wheeling and dealing of negotiating and the feeling that he is doing something worthwhile" were expressing the same kind of satisfaction in meeting a challenge.

Basic level jobs

Basic level jobs were defined as ones where there was no supervisory responsibility. Women occupied a far higher proportion of basic level jobs than did men. This was at its most marked in the administration and finance sections of housing departments where at basic level 85 per cent of the staff were women. Women constituted three quarters of the basic level staff in management and administration and finance although in development and rehabilitation sections they formed only one third of basic level staff. What kind of jobs did they do? Although many of these jobs were on clerical grades only a minority were simply concerned with typing and filing. To illustrate this we will take examples of three jobs commonly found in housing organisations and predominantly occupied by women – telephonists, receptionists and interviewers. Although they are classified as basic level jobs they are very important for they are often the first point of contact for the public.

Telephonists. The first person an applicant comes into contact with in a housing organisation is usually either a telephonist or a receptionist and both observation and the research shows that this is highly likely to be a woman. The telephonist has to deal with a constant stream of incoming calls. Frequently members of the public or tenants calling in do not know who to ask for by name. The telephonist has to try to clarify the nature of the call, make a swift diagnosis and put the call through or advise the caller that they need another number, the district rather than a central office, for example. The caller may have been waiting for some time to get through an already overloaded exchange, or may feel a sense of grievance so may be already aggressive or abusive. It is the telephonist who feels the effect of this aggression. This pattern may be repeated over and over again during one day so that a telephonist who not only has the knowledge to 'sift' calls accurately, but also can deal with difficult callers, is a great asset to a housing organisation. Conversely if the telephonist's work is not done well, callers can be so alienated by the time they get through to the next person that the task of dealing with them is doubly difficult.

Receptionists. Receptionists usually perform a similar 'sifting job' job to the telephonists with the added difficulty that they cannot 'disconnect' if a caller becomes abusive. Often they can see a visible queue of people waiting to be dealt with while the telephonist's 'queue' is invisible. In some organisations receptionists' jobs are combined with other functions, such as dealing with waiting lists or tenancy queries, while in others they perform a purely 'sifting' function, very often having to direct callers where to wait until the appropriate staff member appears. Like the telephonist the receptionist is the first contact with the member of the public, who may have to be told that they have come to the wrong office or at the wrong time or will have to wait. In this situation they are also subject to abuse or, more rarely, physical assault – usually the result of a situation over which they have no control. As one such woman member of staff said "Reception work is very difficult because it is tiring and people want to explain everything to you rather than being referred to someone else," "I try to be as sympathetic as possible but the constant pressure of people waiting and frequent hostility make it difficult."

It is interesting that in general practice the receptionist is also usually a woman and is also in the front line of the service. A government committee stressed the enormous importance of this role.[4] The significance of the person who has initial contact with the public is increasingly recognised. The relationship formed at this point is the one most likely to colour the patient's or client's view of the service.

Interviewing applicants. In most housing organisations applicants for housing are interviewed and the interviewer is often a woman. Applicants may be well informed and arguing for their rights or at the other end of the scale confused, worried, ignorant of 'the system', illiterate or speaking very little English.

The interviewer must try, in a limited space of time, both to get the correct information from the interviewee and to convey accurate information to the interviewee about the organisation's policy or alternative course of action. Not surprisingly the applicant may go away unsatisfied. The interviewer very often goes on after a very short pause to interview the next person. The comment of one such member of staff was that the main task of the job is "thinking up 1001 nice ways to say no".

All these staff, telephonists, receptionists and interviewers are 'basic level' staff. Although these examples are taken from the lettings and 'reception of the public' function these jobs are fairly typical of the jobs one would expect to find a woman doing in a housing organisation. Nevertheless it is important not to forget the variety of jobs in housing organisations even at basic level.

Some women were engaged in the more stereotyped clerical work where they might find less job satisfaction. "My job is unsatisfying, mundane and boring and I never seem to get anything done" said one such woman. "The postholder's main problem is boredom partly because of the nature of the work" was the comment of another. The secretary who "feels that she is not used to her full potential because she is quite capable of replying to letters, for example, without having the answer written out for her; feels that people are not used to having secretaries" was echoing a very common complaint of secretaries.[5]

Some women with basic level jobs have very exacting work. For example, one was responsible for investigating cases of harassment by landlords, trying to arrange a satisfactory outcome but, if this failed, preparing the statements for the legal section for prosecution and appearing in court if necessary. And while most wardens of sheltered accommodation were women so were a number of 'estate officers' or 'housing assistants' who were responsible for management of estates. These would still be classified as basic level jobs unless they had responsibility for directly supervising other staff.

In housing, therefore, it is as true of women's jobs as of men's that the fact that they are 'basic level' or even clerical grade does not mean that they are doing typing, filing or simple figure work or that the jobs are not complicated. One of the most constant characteristics of jobs at this grade is frequent contact with members of the public and the need to exercise a caring and social role.

Summing up

It is now possible to define more clearly the difference in the work which men and women do in housing organisations, not only in terms of grade but also in terms of the nature of the work. Women comprise the majority of the lower grade staff. They also comprise the majority of those in basic level jobs. This means very often that the work is taxing and demanding and in the majority of cases it will involve dealing with people face to face. It will involve applying standard procedures of the organisation but in most cases will provide little opportunity to affect the policies of the organisation or to exercise power in running it.

As we have seen, there are women on the lower rungs of management jobs and these women do have authority over other staff in the day to day running of their sections and may have some input into policy. Their scope is likely to be limited however. When we reach the more senior management and chief officer level, where most of the power and policy making is concentrated, we have seen that there is an even smaller proportion of women. In general as the level of authority within the organisation rises, so the proportion of women decreases. Compared with the other sectors of local government, however, it is only in social services that women are in a relatively better position as chief officers. What factors affect this situation? The survey included questions on three factors which might possibly affect the relative position of men and women – interest in housing as a career, educational qualifications and professional qualifications.

Factors which might affect achievement

Interest in housing as a career

One reason which is sometimes given by senior officers for women's lack of advancement is that women are not so interested in a career as men. At one stage in the *Housing Staff* survey interviewees were asked to agree or disagree with the statement "I'm not the kind of person who has a career in housing". The answers of men and women are compared in Table 5.3.

The responses could be held to show that there was some difference in stated career motivation between the men and women in the sample. 67 per cent of the women felt that they did have a career in housing as compared with 79 per cent of the men. This 10 per cent difference does not seem sufficient however to produce the great disparity in career achievement. Also interpretation of

Table 5.3

"I'm not the kind of person who has a career in housing"

	Men	%	Women	%
Strongly disagree		29		18
Disagree		50		49
Not applicable		8		10
Agree		11		21
Strongly agree		2		2
	(397)	100	(382)	100

Source: Education and Training for Housing Work Project. *Housing Staff* Survey, The City University, 1977.

the results is complicated by the fact that there was also a grade difference in responses to this question. Twice as many clerical staff agreed or agreed strongly with the statement about 'not having a career in housing' than did staff on S.O. grades and above. There is therefore a problem of causation – was the attitude to a career in housing caused by the fact that these respondents were clerical staff or that they were women?

Another question which might help to illustrate different attitudes to career development was one which was intended to cast light on attitudes to training. Respondents were asked to indicate how interested they were in further training and the results are shown below in Table 5.4.

Table 5.4

Interest in further training by men and women

	Men	%	Women	%
Very interested		53		41
Fairly interested		29		32
Indifferent		5		8
Not really interested		5		5
Definitely not		4		5
Not applicable		4		9
	401	100	394	100

Source: Education and Training for Housing Work Project. *Housing Staff* Survey, The City University, 1977.

Here there was not much difference between the attitudes of men and women. Women did seem more 'tepid' in their responses with fewer 'very interested' replies. 73 per cent of the women as opposed to 82 per cent of the men expressed some interest in training. But in housing organisations training has mainly been equated with professional qualifications or at least going away on courses. Both these forms of training might have initially been expected to appeal less to women, particularly married women. Interest in training would therefore seem to indicate an interest in the job which is common to both men and women.

Any differences in motivation seem very minor in comparison to the huge discrepancy between the career patterns of men and women in housing. We therefore turn to another factor which might be responsible for women's lack of advancement – lack of educational qualifications.

Educational qualifications

A striking fact to emerge from *Housing Staff* was that just under one third of the sample held no educational qualifications at all, perhaps an unexpected finding for non manual staff. A further 28 per cent had qualifications up to C.S.E./'O' level/Matriculation (referred from now on as the 'O' level.) Only 16 per cent had a degree or H.N.D./H.N.C. (referred to here onward as 'higher qualifications').

The overall crosstabulation of educational qualification and grade did not show much association between the two factors, except that clerical level staff were definitely less likely to have 'A' level or higher qualifications. However, when the position of women with educational qualifications was compared with that of men, an interesting picture emerged.

In housing departments, for example, 5 per cent of the men holding 'higher qualifications' were on clerical grades while 10 per cent of the similarly qualified women were on clerical grade. This difference increased in A.P. 1–3 grades where 7 per cent of the men and 18 per cent of the women holding higher qualifications were found. Of the men in departments holding higher qualifications 72 per cent were on grades above A.P. 3 compared with only 40 per cent of the women.

Thus on the grade A.P. 4–5 three times as many women had 'higher qualifications' than men and a greater percentage of the men had no qualification or simply 'O' level. The same was true at S.O. grades. Half the men with higher qualifications were on these grades compared with only 20 per cent of the women.

Within the associations there was a similar pattern. Thus 57 per cent of the women with higher qualifications were on A.P. 1–3 grades as compared with 29 per cent of the men. At A.P. 4–5 a considerably larger proportion of men than women had no qualification or only 'O' level and twice as many women as men had higher qualifications. In the senior grades, too, the position in departments held true for associations.

Generally therefore, grade and educational qualification seemed to be more strongly related for men than for women. While the majority of men with higher qualifications had reached S.O. and P.O. grades the majority of women with these qualifications were on A.P. and Clerical grades. If there is a reason why women do not reach the better jobs in housing therefore, it is not because they lack educational qualifications – they are better qualified than men on the same grade. However, although this difference is striking, it might be argued that general educational qualifications are not especially relevant to the work being done in housing. Professional qualifications, on the other hand, should be relevant so in the next section we look at the members of the *Housing Staff* sample who had professional qualifications.

Professional qualifications

The principal qualification specific to housing administration is the Diploma in Housing Management of the Institute of Housing which is now known as the Professional Qualification of the Institute of Housing. In this section we are concerned only with those staff who held the Diploma or its equivalent, in the organisations covered by the City University Survey. Among the 795 staff there were only 51 people who held the Diploma or its equivalent and another 89 who had either passed part or were studying it.

With such a small sample of qualified staff conclusions, especially about sub categories, must be tentative. However the sample gave some interesting pointers. Qualification, not surprisingly, was allied with higher grades – for example, 31 of the 113 staff above P.O. grade were qualified. There were more qualified men than women but not overwhelmingly so – the women formed approximately one third of the qualified staff, the men two thirds. However, while 23 out of the 32 qualified men had reached grades of P.O. and above, only 8 out of the 19 qualified women had done so. This seems to indicate that while professional qualification was in general a help to higher grades it was much less so for women than it was for men.

The sample also indicates that the disproportion in the numbers of professionally qualified men and women is by no means as great as the disproportion in the number of senior posts held. Conclusions from small numbers must, however, be treated with caution. Fortunately there are other records which provide information about qualified staff (though as will be seen they are not entirely reliable).

Conclusions

The evidence from national data and the *Housing Staff* survey, though restricted in scope, gives a fairly clear picture. Women in housing are concentrated in lower grade jobs with little influence. When they achieve higher grade jobs this is more likely to be in housing management. Their lack of achievement is not due to lack of career motivation or lack of educational qualifications. Professional qualifications may help women to achieve higher grades but not as much as they do men.

The general picture of a lack of women in higher grades is common to many occupations. C. Hakim in *Occupational Segregation* discusses both horizontal segregation, where men and women work in different types of occupation, and vertical segregation where men are in higher grade occupations and women in the lower grade. The evidence suggests that both types occur within the housing service. Hakim concludes "despite certain shifts in the sex composition of occupations, there has been no decrease in the overall level of occupational segregation".[6] But what is so striking in the case of housing is that women, at the end of the last century and the first half of this, were in the forefront of housing management: so much so that it was advocated as 'a career for women'. This is hardly what one would conclude from the *Housing Staff* evidence. What caused this change?

58

In order to examine this question we will look back to the beginnings of housing management and start by considering Octavia Hill, the pioneer of housing work for women. We then trace the history of the employment of trained women staff up to the 1970s. In tracing this history, although we are dealing with a small group of qualified staff, we hope to cast light on a number of aspects of women's employment noted in this chapter. These are their relatively better position in housing associations and in housing management and their concentration in jobs with a 'caring' image. In Chapter 9 and the Conclusions we will consider both the reasons for the seeming decline in the position of qualified women and the overall factors which affect women's employment.

References
1. Education and Training for Housing Work Project. *Housing Work,* The City University, 1977, p. 34.
2. Royal Institute of British Architects. 'Earnings Survey report 1977' quoted in the *Architect's Journal,* 12.10.77, p. 688.
3. Quoted in *The Guardian,* 3.6.76.
4. Department of Health and Social Security, The Report of a sub-committee of the Standing Medical Advisory Committee. *The Organisation of Group Practice,* H.M.S.O. 1971.
5. R. Silverstone, *The Office Secretary,* A study of an occupational group of women office workers. Unpublished PhD thesis, The City University 1974, pp. 224–25 and p. 38.
6. C. Hakim. *Occupational Segregation,* Research Paper No. 9, Department of Employment, December 1979, p. 46.

CHAPTER 6

Looking Back – Octavia Hill and the Beginning of Housing Work for Women

"Octavia Hill and Florence Nightingale were the two greatest women of the nineteenth century" declared Lionel Curtis, first honorary Secretary of the National Trust.[1] Octavia's best known biographer Moberly Bell, admits "there must be many who would be ashamed not to know the significance of Florence Nightingale, Dorothea Beale, Josephine Butler or Elizabeth Garrett Anderson, who have only the haziest idea of Octavia's contribution to the national life".[2] Not all modern commentators would agree with these views but there *is* general agreement about two things. Octavia Hill was a pioneer both in developing modern housing management and in encouraging the employment of women in housing. Although other women were influential it was from the work of Octavia Hill and from the helpers whom she trained that the tradition of women in housing work began.

Early influences

Octavia Hill, born in 1838, came from a slightly unusual background for a Victorian middle class woman. Owing to family financial difficulties she had to contribute to her own keep and at only fourteen, was invited to take charge of a workroom for ragged school children. Her experience was thus radically different from that of most ladies of her day who were expected to occupy themselves in genteel pursuits while awaiting the haven of marriage. Unlike many women of her era, throughout most of her life Octavia had to manage her own finances and money was often a worry.

By the time she was sixteen her circle of friends included Ruskin and F. D. Maurice. Maurice started a Working Women's College and in 1856 Octavia was appointed their secretary but continued to take an interest in the child toy makers. By this time her work among the working classes had enlarged her understanding of the way in which they lived and this, and her circle of friends, led her into a number of charitable enterprises.

Housing conditions

The extremely rapid growth of towns in the early Victorian era, the lack of controls on speculators, who put up new cheap buildings for the working classes, and the enormous overcrowding had produced appalling conditions in Victorian working class housing. Social reformers were beginning to become aware of these. The investigation of the Poor Law Commissioners into the sanitary condition of the labouring population demonstrated that this cause should appeal not only to charitable instincts but also to self interest because of the effect of bad sanitary conditions on the incidence and spread of disease.[3]

Efforts were made to remedy this situation through the building of model dwellings. The Metropolitan Association for Improving the Dwellings of the Industrious Classes founded in 1841 aimed to provide "the labouring man with an increase of the comforts and conveniences of life, with full compensation to the capitalist".[4] The Society for Improving the Condition of the Labouring Classes, which began to interest itself in housing in 1844 was not quite so confident of providing large scale housing on this kind of basis. They hoped rather to produce, on a relatively small scale, model dwellings for various types of tenant which would provide an example for others to follow. Employers had also begun to build model towns to house their employees. The 1850s and 60s saw a number of charitable housing ventures including the Peabody Trust which was eventually endowed with £500,000. These efforts, however, could do no more than nibble at the enormous housing problem. In particular they were more successful in housing the 'respectable artisan' than the poorest of the working classes.

The early work

In 1859 the Association for Sanitary Reform was founded, with a slightly different emphasis in its work, in giving more prominence to management. At the first meeting of this society Lord Shaftesbury, the Chairman, "explained how much of the work in its practical detail was specially suited to women, while the legislative must be done by men".[5] At the same meeting Kingsley "maintained that a great deal of the insanitary conditions that prevailed were due to the neglect on the part of the small landlords of small houses, and he hoped that ladies would make it part of their work to influence them as landlords in the welfare of their tenants. He dwelt on the high infantile mortality and the inexorable fate that hung over so many babies. He urged the necessity for women to take up the work because on it the saving of so much infant life depended."[6]

For these reformers the involvement of women in the beginning of housing work was very much an extension of their conventional role in caring for the home and children. A few years later Ruskin was in a position to see these ideas put into practice, by assisting Octavia Hill. Octavia was trying to find housing for some of the female toy makers and pupils in her charge. When it proved difficult to find decent homes she finally decided that the only solution was to become a landlord herself. John Ruskin "came forward with all the money necessary, and took the whole risk of the undertaking upon himself. He showed me, however, that it would be far more useful if it could be made to pay; that a working man ought to be able to pay for his own house; that the outlay upon it ought, therefore, to yield a fair percentage on the capital invested."[7] This combination of economic determinism and concern for the poor was characteristic of the '5 per cent philanthropists'.[8]

Thus at the age of twenty six Octavia became the agent for three tenement houses in Paradise Place, Marylebone. "It should be observed that well built houses were chosen, but they were in a dreadful state of dirt and neglect. . . . The place swarmed with vermin; the papers, black with dirt, hung in long strips from the walls; the drains were stopped, the water supply out of order."[9] Repairs were done but no new appliances installed until the tenants had proved themselves capable of taking care of their property. A regular sum was set aside for repairs. If any remained after breakage and damage had been repaired, at the end of the quarter, each tenant decided in turn in what way the surplus should be spent. This early example of tenant participation in management seems not to have been followed in later ventures.

Growth in the scope of the work

Gradually her work in managing these houses became known and other friends bought houses and handed them over for management. Eighteen months after the original purchase of the houses Octavia could "look back with thankfulness on what she had been able to do. Her scheme had proved financially sound, she had paid 5 per cent on the capital."[10] She had already attracted helpers such as Emma Cons who became head of a band of rent collectors who were being trained in housing work.

As her reputation spread other friends found property for her to manage or offered money for investment. "I have always a book with a long list of people who offer money for investment. I just put down what amount they offer and when I have workers and hear of courts I only run my eye down the list and choose whoever I think will be best to work with and never since 1864 have I had to wait a day for money for houses."[11]

In this informal way the work grew both with cottage properties and blocks in the West End. Early efforts to manage property in working class boroughs were not uniformly successful, partly due to the lack of local help. "In Deptford the task ultimately proved too difficult and Miss Hill did not shrink from relinquishing work which she felt she could not fulfil."[12] In Southwark, however, the work was more successful. A few small properties were acquired and rebuilt and as ground landlords the Ecclesiastical Commissioners facilitated the purchase of building leases by private people interested in Octavia's work.

The Ecclesiastical Commissioners were obviously impressed with this work and after a period of negotiation in 1884 handed over to Octavia a group of old courts to manage and this was quickly followed by another group. The Commissioners, however, retained overall financial control and responsibility for capital expenditure. The result of their experience of this system of management was described by the Secretary of the Ecclesiastical Commissioners in 1919.

"The basis is a business and not a philanthropic one. The following beneficial results are experienced:

Practically no losses of rent and no arrears;

Steady continuance of tenancies;

Repairs and redecorations moderate;

Character and conduct of tenants good;

Absence of quarrels over user of joint rights, e.g., staircases, yards, etc., etc.;

Tenants contented and taking pride in the appearance of their dwellings;

Educative influence beneficial growing out of the association of those responsible for the management of the estate with the social activities of the district."[13]

The association with the Ecclesiastical Commissioners was important because it widened the scope of the work. New blocks of flats and rows of cottages were erected in Southwark and Westminster and other rebuilding schemes begun. Gradually similar schemes were adopted in some provincial towns. As early as 1885 Octavia had been recognised as an authority on working class housing and gave evidence before the *Royal Commission on the Housing of the Working Classes*. Octavia's work was to have increasing influence even in countries overseas and had spread to a wide band of helpers before her death in 1912.

What was the Octavia Hill system?

Octavia Hill herself did not want her practice regarded as any kind of rigid system. As with so many historical figures each generation has made its own interpretation of her contribution and it is often difficult to sort out the facts. There are a few main sources of evidence for her opinions – the practice of her work, a few articles, evidence before the Royal Commission and the 'Letters to Fellow Workers' which she wrote over a period of years. The published volume of her writing is small and this is consistent with her character as a doer rather than a theorist. Octavia's own words bear this out: "I have been asked to add a few words about the homes of the people, but what can I say? There is so much said. Is it not better now just silently to do?"[14]

Her ideas need therefore to be seen from the work which she did as much as from what she wrote. In the following summary both aspects are borne in mind though as far as possible her own words are used as 'supporting testimony'.

She emphasised the importance of *the management of property as a positive contribution to the solution of housing problems*. Much of the emphasis of the time was on sweeping away slums and replacing them with new buildings. This idea of the importance of management is implicit in her whole life's work but was made explicit in her writings. "One can see any day excellent buildings execrably managed, and one may see tumble-down old places of wretched construction both healthier and far more home-like because well managed. And I may confidently say that the distinctive feature of our work has been that of devoting our full strength to management."[15]

She stressed the idea *that both landlord and tenant had obligations which should be performed*. "There is, firstly, the simple fulfilment of a landlady's bounden duties, and uniform demand of the fulfilment of those of the tenants."[16]

She wanted to *tackle the housing problems of the very poorest classes*. When she gave evidence before the *Royal Commission on the Housing of the Working Classes* (1884–85) she was asked, "you feel that artisans and respectable labourers can nowadays be left more or less to themselves, but your work is mainly to reform the tenants that nobody else will touch?" She answered "Yes, the tenants and the houses, one might almost say."[17] In order to do so, however, she felt that personal contact and consideration was needed. "I am certain that you can hunt the poor about from place to place, rout them out of one place and drive them to another; but you will never reach the poor except through people who care about them."[18] Thus she felt it was better to use a gradual approach. "We buy the rooms perfectly teeming with people, and for a few weeks we go on like that; and then we gradually get them to move into larger or to take additional rooms; and we deal with everything gradually in that way."[19]

Her practice was of *housing management as an integrated function*. In the properties managed by Octavia Hill and those she trained the housing manager was responsible for the collection of rent, matters affecting tenants such as allocations, transfers, disputes and at least the routine maintenance of the building. In many ways this follows naturally from the idea of seeking to ensure that the landlord and the tenant fulfil their obligations promptly. It seems likely that the 'landlord' is best placed to achieve this when the relevant functions are under unified control. This basic idea, as we shall see, had many vicissitudes in later history.

Following again naturally from these other practices was *the idea of trained workers to carry out this new type of housing management*. Early on we find much stress on the ideas of 'lady volunteers' but by the end of her life it is clear that she realised paid workers would be needed. "I have been thinking a great deal about how responsible bodies can, in the future, secure such management by trained ladies as has been found helpful in the past. This has turned my attention much more than heretofore to the thought of how to provide more responsible professional workers, for I feel that, however much volunteers may help, it is only to professional workers that responsible and continuous duties can, as a rule, be entrusted especially by large owners or corporations". . . . "Then I realized that my best plan for the future would be not only to train such volunteers as offered and the professional workers whom we required but to train more professional workers than we ourselves can use, and, as occasion offers, to introduce them to owners wishing to retain small tenements in their own hands and to be represented in them by a kind of manager not hitherto existing". . . .

"We can all remember how the training of nurses and of teachers has raised the standard. . . . The same change might be hoped for in the character of the management of dwellings let to the poor."[20]

Housing management as practiced by Octavia Hill was however an *authoritarian function* with firm ideas of the poor as people who needed to be 'trained' and 'guided'. This extended to the use of eviction against tenants who did not pay their rent or were otherwise 'unsatisfactory'.

"I do not say I will not have drunkards, I have quantities of drunkards; but everything depends upon whether I think the drunkard will be better for being sent away or not. It is a tremendous despotism, but it is exercised with a view of bringing out the powers of the people, and treating them as responsible for themselves within certain limits."[21]

Her beliefs were strongly in the laissez faire tradition – not accepting the need to remedy poverty as such and firmly opposed to the advancement of state intervention in all spheres including housing. Consistent with a view of poverty as the responsibility of the individual concerned, and a rejection of 'almsgiving' as whittling away that responsibility, was her opposition to state intervention in social work or housing construction. She felt that such intervention would weaken the ability of the private builder to cope and the responsibility for individual action which she held so important. "I should be sorry to see the State, or the parishes, or the Corporation take up construction. . . . I should leave the construction to individual action, and to building companies. . . ."[22] "I think it (land) is better held in general by individuals. I do not think corporate bodies are good builders, and I do not think they are good managers, so far as I know them. . . ."[23]

She emphasised the value of small houses and existing communities. While some of these ideas are very far from current trends of thought others seem to have come full circle. For example she emphasised the value of keeping small cottages and preserving existing communities. Though agreeing that the construction of 'blocks' might be necessary when buildings had gone beyond repair she was acutely aware of the disadvantages of this form of housing. She criticised 'blocks' for their lack of privacy, for the discomfort caused to 'quiet' tenants by noise and because she felt that most families should have some private garden space. "She said to us: 'Even a third rate house with a backyard of its own is better than the modern flats which the London County Council is now building, because when the tenant can command his own front door and staircase, he can preserve the unity of his family.'" . . . "She determined . . . to build model cottages in which each tenant would command his own front door and staircase, and if possible a tiny separate garden for each."[24]

Assessments of Octavia Hill's work

There has been considerable divergence in modern assessments of Octavia Hill's work. At the beginning of the chapter two very flattering views were presented. Not many modern commentators would agree with them. More would agree with Owen. "Of all the later Victorians few are more baffling to a twentieth century interpreter. Her achievements were formidable and some of them . . . can be praised unreservedly. But of the work into which she put her greatest energy . . . one must speak in more qualified terms. Though her contemporaries regarded her as an oracle on working class housing and her accomplishments in the field were staggering, they no longer command unquestioning admiration. . . . Her own work placed Octavia Hill not in the vanguard of the main army but, one might almost say, in charge of a diversionary operation."[25]

Two particular aspects of Octavia Hill's attitudes stick in the throat of such modern commentators. The first is her outspoken opposition to public intervention in housing. The second is her 'moralistic' and 'despotic' attitude to the working classes and to tenants of public housing in particular. Tarn[26] attacks her sharply "Whatever her initial success, the solution was never more than a palliative." However his accusation that she was "a reactionary as far as physical realities were concerned: she did not take a long term view of the problems and gave her support to immediate action" is not entirely justified in that Octavia's predictions about the difficulties for families in blocks of flats have proved only too accurate over the last few years.

Such critics hold particularly that in her approach Octavia Hill was ignoring the real roots of the housing problem in the widespread poverty of the 'lower classes'. Thus Beatrice Webb concluded. "The lady collectors are an altogether superficial thing. Undoubtedly their gentleness and kindness brings light into many homes: but what are they in the face of this collective brutality, heaped up together in infectious contact; adding to each other's dirt, physical and moral?"[27]

History, as always, is the reinterpretation of the past in terms of the present. Commentators find it unacceptable that Octavia held views which even in her own time were already becoming outdated. "If they were the achievements of a woman of impressive stature, they were also expressions of a social outlook that today is almost incomprehensible and even in the 1880's and '90's was being vigorously challenged."[28] The future was to lie with the expansion of state intervention in housing. Does this mean that the whole of Octavia Hill's work was irrelevant? When reviewing her work today it is also important to consider which aspects of her 'system' Octavia herself would have thought essential and which were a product of the circumstances of the time. Octavia did not want to lay down any rigid system and because of this she even resisted the idea of an association "My friends know that it has never seemed to me well to form any association whether of the owners of the various dwellings we manage, or of ourselves the workers who manage. . . . Societies cannot create a spirit. . . . All we can do is, where the spirit exists, to try to qualify workers by giving them training, and then link them with an owner and group of tenants."[29] She saw the need for the development of ideas.

It is here that modern commentators may have been less kind to Octavia Hill than to other pioneers and this harshness may arise partly from the very political nature of the housing service. It seems possible for commentators to acknowledge, for example, that Florence Nightingale was a domineering and dictatorial woman with little tolerance for the ideas of others: to admit that many of Shaftsbury's ideas were decidedly conservative and that Chadwick, one of the great pioneers of public health, was completely mistaken about the origin and appropriate policy for typhoid, and yet to accept the contribution which each of these made to social policy.

In the same way it should be possible to identify the positive contributions made by Octavia Hill while acknowledging the aspects described above. The positive contributions are the idea that the management of property is worthy of attention and the construction of new dwellings is not of itself enough: the idea of an integrated estate management which does not separate 'welfare' from other functions and the idea of training staff to carry out this work. Other aspects of her work can also still be admired – the stress on the need for community facilities and play space for children and the emphasis on the perils of wholesale demolition which has been strongly re-echoed in the 1970s.

Walton holds that aspects of Octavia Hill's individualism made a positive contribution. "In social work there have been notable contributions by women which have particularly emphasised the value of the individual and his or her needs in the face of a perplexing and often harmful social environment. A link can be traced from Octavia Hill, Mary Carpenter and Josephine Butler which . . . has influenced the whole of social work by the embodiment of ideals and values in the pattern of social work training evolved in this country . . . it can be argued that it has been a particular contribution of women in social work to nurture these ideals in action and so maintain a countervailing balance against impersonal bureaucratisation of services."[30]

Other influential women

Thus the contribution which Octavia Hill made to the development of housing is an ambiguous one. Many other women also contributed to the movement for the improvement of the housing of the working classes, Beatrice Webb worked in 'Octavia Hill' type management with Ella Pycroft who managed dwellings for the East End Dwellings Company. Emma Cons, later the founder of the 'Old Vic', worked with Octavia Hill in the early days though she later differed over methods. Other women unconnected with this group, such as Eleanor Rathbone, waged war on both poverty and poor housing conditions.

In an earlier period Angela Burdett-Coutts had been one of the innovators in building model dwellings. After taking the advice of Octavia Hill's grandfather, Dr Southwood Smith, who was an authority on public health, she had constructed Columbia Square in Bethnal Green. She insisted on gas and water being laid on and a laundry and drying space with a "huge spin dryer" on the top floor, even though some critics felt these were "unnecessary luxuries" for the poor.[31] But although she maintained an interest in housing she did not build up a sustained body of work.

Octavia Hill, however, is outstanding as the person who introduced women to systematic employment in housing work. As will be seen in a later chapter, the kind of work involved in collecting rents, keeping accounts, ordering and supervising repairs, does not conform to stereotyped ideas about the nature of women's work. Even enlightened contemporaries such as Beatrice Webb commented that it required characteristics which they did not normally associate with women. "These governing and guiding women may become important factors if they increase as they have done lately; women who give up their own lives to the management of men; their whole energy, body and mind, absorbed in it. Unlike the learned woman, the emotional part of their nature is fully developed; their sympathy almost painfully active. . . . They have the dignity of habitual authority; often they have the narrow mindedness and social gaucherie due to complete absorption, physical and mental, in one set of feelings and ideas."[32] Beatrice Webb here makes an interesting distinction between the learned woman – presumably the academic who to most people represented the 'new woman' – and the kind of women involved in management work. Up to this day housing management still requires a blend of practical and planning abilities which is not the same as academic attainment.

Many of the women trained by Octavia Hill or associated with her in this work were able to develop qualities which were not always recognised in Victorian women. What is more this employment did not collapse on Octavia's death, but the women concerned eventually joined together to form a cohesive group. There were still many obstacles to meet before women could feel secure in this field of employment and it may be that some of these continue to the present day. Nevertheless the credit for pioneering the employment of women in housing must be given to Octavia Hill.

References
1. W. T. Hill. *Octavia Hill,* Hutchinson, 1956, p. 183.
2. E. Moberly Bell. *Octavia Hill,* Constable & Co. 1942, p. 97.
3. Poor Law Commission. *4th Annual Report,* 1838.
4. C. Gatliff. 'On Improved Dwellings and their Beneficial effect on Health and Morals, and suggestions for their extension.' *Journal of the Statistical Society,* March 1875.
5. M. E. Tabor. *Octavia Hill,* The Sheldon Press, 1927, p. 12.
6. *Ibid.*
7. O. Hill. *Homes of the London Poor,* Macmillan and Co. London 1875, pp. 15–16.
8. See D. Owen. *English Philanthropy,* Harvard University Press, 1956, Chap. XIV 'Philanthropy and Five Per Cent'.
9. O. Hill. *op cit.* p. 17.
10. E. Moberly Bell. *Octavia Hill,* Constable and Co. 1942, p. 97.
11. *Ibid.* p. 117.
12. J. M. Upcott. 'Women House Property Managers', *Building News,* (date unknown), p. 17.
13. *Ibid.* p. 23.
14. Octavia Hill. 'Colour, Space and Music for the People' address to The Kyrle Society, *The Nineteenth Century,* May 1884, pp. 741–52.
15. Octavia Hill. Letter to my Fellow Workers 1897, quoted in *House Property and Its Management,* Ed. M. Jeffery, E. Neville, George Allen and Unwin, 1921, p. 17.
16. Octavia Hill. *Homes of the London Poor, op. cit.* p. 30.
17. Royal Commission on the Housing of the Working Classes (1885), *Minutes of Evidence,* p. 304.
18. W. T. Hill. *op. cit.,* p. 183.
19. Royal Commission on the Housing of the Working Classes (1885), *Minutes of Evidence,* p. 297.
20. O. Hill quoted in *House Property and Its Management, op. cit.,* pp. 64–65.
21. Royal Commission on the Housing of the Working Classes (1885), *Minutes of Evidence,* p. 297.
22. *Ibid,* p. 295.
23. *Ibid,* p. 292.
24. W. T. Hill, *op. cit.,* p. 14.

25. D. Owen, *op. cit.,* p. 387.
26. J. N. Tarn. *Working Class Housing in Nineteenth Century Britain,* Lund Humphries, 1971, p. 25.
27. B. Webb. *My Apprenticeship,* Penguin, 1971, pp. 282–83.
28. D. Owen. *op. cit.,* p. 387.
29. Octavia Hill. *Management of Houses for the Poor,* Charity Organisation Society Occasional Papers No. 7 Series, January 1889.
30. R. G. Walton. *Women in Social Work,* Routledge and Kegan Paul, 1975, p. 261.
31. E. Healey. *Lady Unknown, The Life of Angela Burdett-Coutts,* London, 1978, p. 122.
32. B. Webb, *op. cit.,* p. 273.

CHAPTER 7

The Rise of a Women's Professional Housing Society, 1912–1938

The beginning of an Association of Women Housing Managers

"When I am gone, I hope my friends will not try to carry out any special system, or to blindly follow the track which I have trodden. New circumstances require various efforts; and it is the spirit, not the dead form that should be perpetuated."[1]

These much quoted words were spoken by Octavia Hill, who had been very concerned about handing on her work to suitably trained staff. "Miss Hill had, before her death in August, 1912, so organised her work that each manager trained by her should be able to carry on independently when she was gone."[2] Harriet Yorke, a close friend and a fellow worker with Octavia Hill for 30 years continued to be a personal link between many of the workers. However, Octavia Hill's own insistence against being associated with any particular group perhaps delayed the growth of a more formalised association. The next step forward was not so much in the field of association as in employment.

During the 1914–18 war the Ministry of Munitions acquired or built large amounts of housing. At the beginning some suffered from bad management and various problems arose. Some of the officers in the Ministry knew of Octavia Hill's work and suggested the employment of women managers, one of whom (Miss Lumsden) eventually obtained an advisory post in the Ministry itself. "The value of the work was shown by the great improvement in standards and the avoidance of the rent strikes which were prevalent at the end of the war."[3] Miss Lumsden, at the Ministry, devised a training scheme to ensure the continuance of this type of management. This, however, attracted the notice of the press and a widespread suspicion arose that the returning men would be kept out of these jobs by women. The women managers decided, in these circumstances, that it would be unwise to remain in their posts and all resigned, although, in view of the proven value of their work the Department would have been glad to have retained them.[4]

Although the venture therefore resulted in a reversal to traditional roles it had demonstrated that women were capable of taking on large scale activities under difficult circumstances. Also, in 1916, some of the trained women had met together to discuss war work and this had resulted in the formation of the Association of Women Housing Workers, later to become the Association of

Women House Property Managers. It had then a membership of fifty and a subscription of 2s. 6d. per year. It included not only those who had been on Octavia Hill's staff but women who had in the past collaborated with her. It had a council and an executive committee and a training scheme combining practical and theoretical training with attendance at lectures, culminating in an examination for an assistant's certificate after a year's work and a manager's certificate after two more years of satisfactory work. The objects were:

(1) To unite all engaged in housing work.
(2) To have a representative body to which all interested in housing work might apply.
(3) To arrange for the training of workers and promote the advancement of the knowledge necessary for the efficient management of house property."[5]

The first women's 'professional association' in housing had arrived. It remained small, however.

Meanwhile, another important advance had been made in the sphere of employment. In 1916 the Commissioners of Woods and Forests (later the Crown Estate Commissioners) had placed one house with a trained woman manager. Then other houses were added and ultimately the 2,000 tenancies of their Cumberland Market Estate were under the management of Miss Jeffery, who had been trained in the 'Octavia Hill system'.

The July 1920 issue of *Housing,* the official journal of the Ministry of Health, concentrated on management. With its introductory statement, "The success of working class property depends very largely on its management" it foreshadows many worthy official documents. It goes on to a number of equally enlightened views "Proper management will require a person specially skilled and trained for the work. . . . The manager must be given ample authority. . . . The work will require training. There is at present lack of opportunity for it. Little is done except by the Association of Women House Property Managers, who have rendered such admirable service in redeeming unfit property. There will have to be more facilities for training if the needs are to be met. . . ." Property management is a profession as well adapted to women as to men.[6]

Miss Jeffery's office at Cumberland Market became an important training ground for new managers. Irene Barclay, who started work in this office, recorded how Miss Jeffery encouraged her and Miss Perry to qualify as surveyors once the *Sex Disqualification (Removal) Act* 1919 made this possible. "A good deal of foolish fuss was made of us as the first Women Surveyors. . . ."[7] Mrs Barclay went on to became the Secretary of the St. Pancras Housing Association. This was one of a number of housing societies and associations registered under the *Industrial and Provident Societies Act 1893*, which grew up in the 1920s and 1930s.

Women get a foothold in local government

As far as the local authorities, now becoming major providers of housing, were concerned, acceptance of women housing managers was more doubtful. There were at the end of the war signs of a movement to appoint trained women to estate management posts in local government – two members from the Association went to Birmingham and in 1921 Amersham Rural District Council appointed a member of the Society, Miss Geldard, as housing manager but "with no actual adoption of the principles derived from Octavia Hill".[8] In 1925 The Town Clerk of Chesterfield, Mr (later Sir) Parker Morris, conducted members of his housing committee to the Crown Estate Commissioners' estate at Cumberland Market. The committee members were so impressed that they appointed Miss Upcott to manage a specially difficult estate, reporting direct to the housing committee. (Miss Upcott had worked with Octavia Hill and for the first four years after Octavia Hill's death had helped Miss Yorke to manage the smaller outlying properties whose management had not been devolved.) This appointment led to similar appointments (of younger workers trained by the London managers) at Walsall, Chester, West Bromwich, Stockton on Tees and Rotherham. In 1928, Leeds approved the introduction of the 'Octavia Hill system' and in the following year appointed a housing manager and two women assistants to look after property in the Quarry Hill area along with part of the Middleton Estate. However, the appointment of women was attacked in council. Despite this initial opposition, the appointment of a woman manager started a tradition of management which was to continue in Leeds almost up to the present day. Women had thus gained a foothold in municipal housing employment, but only a small one. In a number of cases, as in Rotherham, the women managers were used for especially difficult estates or areas whilst the remainder of the properties were managed in a different way.

From the increase of these posts arose the idea of a conference of women municipal managers and this was successfully carried out by Miss Upcott in 1928. This conference, however, emphasised the fact that a division had come about in the professional grouping of Octavia Hill trained women. We have mentioned earlier the foundation of the Association of Women House Property Managers. Miss Jeffery had in 1928 formed the 'Octavia Hill Club' from among the considerable number of those she had trained, many of whom were prepared to fill the new municipal posts in the provinces. The conference of municipal managers was yet a third group which cut across the other two. The need for unity was strongly felt and negotiations between the three groups began. Finally, in 1932, a constitution was agreed by all three bodies. It was agreed that anyone who had done bona-fide housing work under Octavia Hill should enjoy equal eligibility with the new professional managers. 'The Society of Women Housing Estate Officers' (S.W.H.E.M.) which was then formed continued in continuous existence under different names until 1965 when it amalgamated with the Institute of Housing. By 1933 it had a small office in Victoria Street, London, and a full time secretary.

After 1932 women had a unified professional body to represent them, but all was not plain sailing. Local authorities were to be the great area of expansion of social housing but, despite the exhortations of the Ministry of

Health, many continued to split their housing management functions among a number of departments. By 1935 only 17 of the local authorities had appointed chief officers or housing managers be they men or women. Even those prepared to appoint managers were unwilling to appoint women to the posts. In 1936, Liverpool Corporation housing committee appointed Jean Thompson, one of the Association's members, as its estates manager, but rescinded the appointment on the grounds that she would be in charge of men. Questions were asked in the House of Commons, and in the *Municipal Journal* Eleanor Rathbone contrasted local government attitudes with those of the civil service. She branded town halls as 'reactionary', although she admitted that even in the civil service "full equality of opportunity has not been secured".[9] By this time, 46 women managers were employed in local government controlling 23,000 tenancies between them. This move into local government, though small, was seen by the Association as "the most notable development of the last ten years". Moreover comparable women managers also controlled 2,500 properties for the Church Commissioners, 2,000 for the Crown Commissioners and 6,000 for private owners and trusts.[10] The role of women in estate management was however questioned both on grounds of practice and of principle – an argument which we will consider in more detail in Chapter 9.

The Women's Professional Association 1933–38

Covering the period from 1933 onwards the minutes, reports and bulletins of the Society provide a picture of their range of activity. We will first of all consider their attitude to the employment of women both generally and in housing management and then their training scheme and other activities.

Comparable data is not available for the Institute but we shall conclude this chapter with a 'snapshot' of the views of the Society and the Institute as they were in 1937–38.

The employment of women

The Society joined with other bodies which were trying to improve the status of women. In 1933, for example, they sent representatives to the National Council of Women and this representation was continued through the period. In October 1933 "The Society gave its support to a mass meeting for the right of married women to earn."[11]

In 1936 the Society sent a representative with the Women's Engineering Society to the House of Commons. It participated in a Women's National Exhibition in 1937. In 1935 the Society affiliated to the Women's Employment Federation. The National Council of Women invited a representative from the Society "in relation to the forthcoming enquiry by the League of Nations into the status of women in different countries". Miss Upcott attended and it was agreed that she should state:

(1) "That the particular aspect of the status of women in which the Society is interested is the economic;

(2) That the aim of the Society is to secure equality of opportunity for women in the profession of housing estate management."[12]

This clear statement of their principles was matched by the Society's practice. They were obviously anxious that women should not be used as cheap labour to substitute for men and to avoid as far as possible women being used as mere 'welfare assistants'. They tried to ensure that appointment of a member of the Society went hand in hand with reforms in the system of estate management to introduce more unified arrangements giving adequate control to the housing manager. Thus, for example, in 1934 "Except for one or two minor alterations, the Chelsea Council accepted the conditions of service drawn up by the sub-committee of the Society of Women Housing Estate Managers and the post of Manager was circulated on the agreed terms to members of S.W.H.E.M. only."[13]

Similarly in January 1934 the Society's Council agreed "That the advertisement for a woman rent collector at Lincoln be circulated to members with the recommendation by the Council that they should only accept the post at a salary of £225 rising by £25 to £250 at the end of the year and should state this in their application."[14] There are frequent references to posts advertised at salaries which were too low. A formal protest was made by the Society at their Annual Provincial Conference in 1935 about the action of Liverpool City Council in refusing to confirm Miss Jean Thompson's appointment.

The Society was active in propaganda for the employment of women in housing. It canvassed the universities and women's organisations with a leaflet describing the work of trained women housing managers. Opportunities were often taken when posts were advertised or contact made with local authorities or trusts to explain to them the advantages of housing management as practised by the Society. Neither were journals overlooked. For example, in November 1939 the minutes recorded that Mrs Barclay had written an article for the *New Statesman*, Miss Tabor one for *Women's Magazine* in response to a request and Miss Thompson one after a request from *Public Administration*.

Training

From its beginning the Society continued Octavia Hill's insistence on the adequate training of staff. In 1933 an examination was instituted in the form of the 'Women House Property Managers' Certificate of the Chartered Surveyors' Institution'. This continued to be the qualification for Society members up till the 1960s, though some went on to take the full Surveyors qualification. But close attention was also given to practical training. In 1933 it was decided "that students who have passed through the course laid down for them to the satisfaction of the Training Sub-Committee shall be recommended to the Council for a certificate as a qualified worker".[15] The progress of students was often discussed in detail by the Training sub-committee and they would insist on further training and practical experience if they felt that a student's standard was not adequate. Only certain offices were approved for training and the 'training managers', as they were known, were actively involved in the many discussions which took place on alterations in the form and content of training. In 1936 there was the proposal to the Chartered Surveyors Institute that revision of the Women House Property Managers certificate be postponed for one year. Later there was discussion of the possibility of 'an assistant's certificate', a proposal which was to recur regularly in both Society and Institute.

General housing activities

For the Society concern over the organisation of housing management did not preclude concern over general housing matters. In 1935, for example, the organising secretary of the Over Thirty Association approached the secretary to raise the question of housing accommodation for single working women. It was agreed to inform her that S.W.H.E.M. "viewed with sympathy any endeavour to meet this need".[16]

In April 1936 there was agreement to a resolution submitted by Miss Upcott and Miss Galton to the National Council of Women "To urge on Housing Authorities, Public Utility Societies and private owners the necessity of providing, in connection with re-housing, an adequate minimum of square yards per family of play space for young children adjoining the buildings and of play space for older children near to these buildings."[17] A concern with open space and play facilities was to be a continuing interest, particularly with certain members of the Society, well into the post war years.

The Institute of Housing

In 1931 another group of housing staff, mostly employed in local authorities, had joined together to form an association. Initially the strength of this group was in the Midlands. From the beginning its membership was predominantly, though not exclusively, male. (For example the 1936 Council, the first recorded, was all male and the first woman executive member was not elected until 1939.) Also no specific conditions about training or qualifications were laid on its members. This represented therefore a very different tradition from that of S.W.H.E.M. It was originally called the Institute of Housing Administration, later changing to the Institute of Housing.

In the first years membership of both organisations was not seen as being incompatible and a few women gained positions in the Institute.[18] However, in January 1936 following letters from members (contents unfortunately unknown) we read in the minutes:

"That in view of the facts which have been brought to light Council is of the opinion that membership of the Institute of Housing Administration is rapidly becoming incompatible with membership of the S.W.H.E.M. Members of the latter body are, therefore, asked to consult together as the most effective moment to resign in a body from the I.H.A."[19]

At a meeting on 3rd May 1936 the members of the Society who were also members of the Institute met and decided that they would resign from the Institute within the next fortnight. From this time forward until the post war years the two bodies pursued separate paths but a small overlap of membership continued.

The two rival organisations: Institute and Society in 1938

In view of the limited amount of material available, especially on the Institute, at this time, it is useful to obtain a kind of 'snapshot' caused by their appearance to give evidence to a government body.

The Central Housing Advisory Committee had set up a sub-committee specifically concerned with housing management and housing associations. In 1935, its minutes note that "The Minister had recently received a deputation from the Institute of Housing Administration which was in a sense a rival body to the Society of Women Housing Estate Managers, though the methods and management advocated by the two bodies differed in certain respects. The Institute had asked to be directly represented on the Advisory Committee." The Sub-committee decided to ask both bodies to give evidence but S.W.H.E.M. as "the older and better known body" to be asked to appear first.[20]

Nevertheless it is interesting to note the relative weakness of both bodies. Sir Miles Mitchell (a Manchester Alderman and a member of the sub-committee) writing to Lord Balfour of Burghley (the chairman of the sub-committee) says of the draft report, "I think here too much prominence is given to these two societies for instance so far as I know, the Housing Directors of Liverpool, Leeds and Manchester and probably many others are not connected with either of these two organisations."[21]

The evidence given by the two bodies does however cast an interesting light on their situation at the time.

Membership

The Society had in 1936 134 qualified members, 62 of whom worked for municipal employers and 72 for non-municipal employers. Membership was limited to those who had worked with Octavia Hill and her associates plus those who had later been trained in approved offices. The Institute had a membership of 261 but "not limited to officials engaged in local government nor to housing managers as such". Borough Treasurers and Medical Officers of Health responsible for housing were accepted. But applications "for example from minor officials of small local authorities" had been refused.[22] They could not say how many of the 261 were Chief Officers.

Housing management practice

The evidence given to the committee includes a detailed account of the "working of the Octavia Hill system in the County Borough of Rotherham" by Miss Jean Thompson, who as we have seen, was appointed housing manager in 1928. "The women managers work in administrative control of the estates and at the same time in direct touch with the tenants."[23] Work handled included rent collection, court work, maintenance of properties including ordering and checking the work and accounts of direct labour staff, applications and tenancies, rehousing, social and educational work, committee work and relations with other departments.

In contrast to the comprehensive scope of the work handled by the women managers at Rotherham it is interesting to note the kind of work which the

Institute considered suitable for women. After describing the various possible types of housing official responsible for what would today be called more or less 'comprehensive' duties it goes on to discuss 'welfare work'. "The ideal which we would wish to see", was that each municipal estate should have a 'Woman Welfare Worker' responsible to the Housing Manager. It was considered advantageous that she lived on the estate. She should have a knowledge of the social services, "be capable of teaching cleanliness . . . homely hints such as the making of curtains . . . be of the motherly or matronly type with a definite love of welfare work".[24]

The Society of Women Housing Managers would have none of it. When it was suggested at the Committee that their training might be combined with that of hospital almoners, the reply was "the members of the Society felt more kinship with surveyors and architects, the subjects of whose examinations were to some extent adopted as a basis for the Women House Property Managers Certificate of the Chartered Surveyors Institution".[25]

There was also some difference between the Society and the Institute about the integration of 'welfare' with 'management'. For the Society "The whole of the administrative activities of the department are recognised as giving almost constant opportunity for social and educational work in the broadest sense. The time devoted to this cannot be separated from other work, nor is it seen as a separate section."[26] The same person who had the day-to-day contact with tenants in collecting the rents was also the person who dealt with the repairs and the 'welfare' side of the work. This meant that a trained 'Octavia Hill' manager might be in charge of about 350 properties as at Rotherham. Under other systems a rent collector might be in charge of a larger number of properties but of course a number of other people often in other departments, would have to carry out the functions other than rent collection. The apparent cheapness of the 'rent collector system' was a matter for argument and remained so into the post war years. As indicated earlier, the Institute accepted the idea that the person dealing with welfare might be someone other than the person dealing with management.

In a number of matters, however, there was consensus between at least the written views of the Society and the Institute. Not surprisingly both supported the view that at least the main housing management functions should be in one department. By 1938 both were advocating that the person in charge needed specific training and qualification. The Society had its long established training scheme; the Institute was about to introduce an examination.

Jean Thompson's evidence continues that personal emphasis which we discussed in the previous chapter. "The staff is interested in the tenants as *individuals* rather than in the mass."[27] She also stressed the link between allocations and management. "Future social work with the *tenant* begins with the *applicant* and a carefully thought out approach in the preliminary relations can do much to create the right spirit which is the basis of good management."[28] Much of what she has to say about this we find repeated forty years later in reports based on the D.O.E.'s research on 'Difficult-to-Let Estates'.[29]

By 1938 therefore, both the Society and the Institute were achieving some recognition. But both were in a weak position. In many local authorities the management of council properties was still considered to be something which could be farmed out to numerous departments. Despite official exhortation over nearly twenty years many had still not unified their housing functions, let alone appointed trained managers. The membership of both associations taken together was less than 500. The Society at that stage had its qualified membership fairly evenly split between municipal and other owners. The Institute's strength was still in local government which was to remain the main area of expansion for many years, though some of the large housing trusts were also represented.

References

1. Octavia Hill, quoted in M. E. Tabor. *Octavia Hill,* The Sheldon Press, London, 1927, p. 32.
2. J. M. Upcott. 'Fellow Workers 1912–1932', *Society of Housing Managers Quarterly Journal,* October 1962, p. 5.
3. J. M. Upcott. *op. cit.,* p. 6.
4. *Ibid.,* p. 6.
5. J. M. Upcott. 'Women House Property Managers', *Building News,* 1923, pp. 32–33.
6. Ministry of Health Housing Department, *Housing,* July 1920, p. 1.
7. I. Barclay. 'Property Management' (an essay in *The Road to Success),* Ed. M. I. Cole. Society of Women Housing Estate Managers, date missing, p. 4.
8. J. M. Upcott. *op. cit.,* p. 6.
9. E. Rathbone. 'A Woman's View of the Local Government Service,' *The Municipal Journal,* May 3rd 1935, p. 734.
10. E. Murray. 'Housing Management is Ideally Women's Work,' *The Municipal Journal and Public Works Engineer,* September 6th 1935, p. 1611.
11. Society of Women Housing Estate Managers. *Minutes,* October 1933.
12. S.W.H.E.M., *Minutes,* 3.1.1936.
13. S.W.H.E.M., *Minutes,* 14.4.1934.
14. S.W.H.E.M., *Minutes,* January 1934.
15. S.W.H.E.M., Minutes of Special General Meeting, 6.5.1933.
16. S.W.H.E.M., *Minutes,* 16.11.1935.
17. Ibid. April 1936.
18. *Ibid.* 14.4.1934.
19. *Ibid.* 3.1.1936.
20. C.H.A.C. sub-committee on the Management of Estates, *Minutes,* April 22nd 1935, p. 4 (Public Record Office (P.R.O.) H.L.G./37/4), p. 4.
21. Miles Mitchell, letter to Lord Balfour, 28.2.1938.
22. Institute of Housing. *Evidence* to the C.H.A.C. sub-committee on housing associations and housing management, October 29th, 1936.
23. J. Thompson. *Memorandum on the detailed working of the Octavia Hill system in the County Borough of Rotherham* (P.R.O. H.L.G. 375), p. 1.
24. I.O.H. *Evidence given before special sub-committee at the M.O.H. Estates management of houses erected for the working classes* P.R.O. H.L.G. 375), p. 10.
25. S.W.H.M. *Evidence to C.H.A.C. sub-committee* P.R.O. H.L.G. 37 4).
26. J. Thompson. *op. cit.,* p. 2.
27. *Ibid.* p. 1.
28. *Ibid.*p. 2.
29. S. Wilson and M. Burbidge. 'An Investigation of Difficult to Let Housing', *Housing Review* July-August 1978, pp. 100–104.

CHAPTER 8

The War Years to the Mid Sixties

These thirty years saw many changes for women in the housing service. First came World War Two which brought women into new positions of responsibility. Then followed a period when the Society of Women Housing Managers played an important role in putting forward their views on management and training. But they failed to gain the same expansion in membership as that achieved by the Institute of Housing. After much heart-searching the two organisations amalgamated in 1965.

In this chapter and the succeeding ones a number of quotations are given from interviews with members of the committee which dealt with the unification between the Society and the Institute. All unascribed quotations will come from this group; quotations are only ascribed when the context does not make it clear whether the quotation comes from an 'Institute' or 'Society' interviewee or if it comes from another source. The way in which these interviews were carried out is described in more detail in the Appendix.

The war years

The Second World War brought women many opportunities to do difficult, and often dangerous, jobs and to shoulder a great deal of responsibility. People with housing management experience found extra calls on their services; thus, the January 1941 Bulletin records "Many enquiries have been received during the past six months from local authorities and other landlords wishing to employ women to replace members of their housing staff who have been called up for military service. Since the Blitzkrieg began there have also been enquiries about the employment of some members as rehousing or Billeting Officers in bombed areas; some managers are combining these duties with their usual work."[1]

As in the First World War, a number of women worked as housing managers for the Ministry of Supply, looking after the housing erected for the workers in munitions factories dispersed to the provinces for security reasons. A number of the interviewees had been drawn into this work from other housing jobs. One at least found the atmosphere a welcome change from the somewhat reluctant acceptance of women housing managers in local government. "This was one of the good things about the Ministry of Supply, you went to a factory to take up a job and they said 'Oh, you know about housing, thank goodness, here's the files, here you are, anything you want just ask us, goodbye . . .' it wasn't a case of your wanting to do the job, it was a case of their wanting you to do the job" (Society interviewee).

The difficulties these women faced would have daunted many. Houses that had been demolished or badly damaged, problems over getting repairs done, evacuation, requisitioning, the growing shortage of housing and the absence of staff who had been called up were only some of the problems which had to be tackled. Surprisingly little attention seems to have been given by historians of housing to the conditions of housing during this period. For example, Burnett's *Social History of Housing* stops in 1939 and begins again in 1945.[2] Perhaps one reason for this neglect is that most histories of housing concentrate on building: the administration of housing, apart from legislation, is often overlooked. Possibly this has something to do with the fact that at least until the end of the war period this was so much the province of women.

Discussions about the employment of women in housing continued. In 1944 the Society discussed the admission of men to training but decided against this "in view of the present position of women in the public services". In Scotland, "Miss Pollock had addressed the Edinburgh Social Union . . . reported that there was a strong undercurrent of opposition among factors and local government officials and that approach to local authorities would be almost impossible until the Department of Health had adopted a positive attitude towards the question of housing management."[3] (For many years to come the prospects for the employment of women housing managers in Scotland were to remain even more difficult than they were in England.)

With the coming of peace the emphasis was on making up the devastation of war by building as many houses as soon as possible. Because the major programme of housebuilding was in the public sector employment in local authority housing increased significantly. Membership of the Institute grew at a faster rate than that of the Society.

The Institute

In 1946 the Institute records show that it had 666 members (including 206 students). Applications were increasing "particularly from persons released from H.M. forces".[4] In the next couple of years a very rapid increase in membership occurred (see Figure 8.1). Membership was at this stage not limited to those qualified or trained in any particular way. In 1946 the decision was taken to limit election to membership to persons qualified by examination. Though it was clear this would slow recruitment it was felt that "by the adoption of this new policy the prestige of the Institute and the status of its members will be enhanced".[5] As Figure 8.1 shows the introduction of this restriction did make numbers much more static for a while. But the increase which had occurred before its introduction meant that by the 1950s the Institute was much larger than the Society. At this stage the Institute was running a 'Housing Estate Management' examination. In 1946 a 'Woman Welfare Officers Certificate Examination' was introduced but this was dropped in 1948 as there were few examinees.

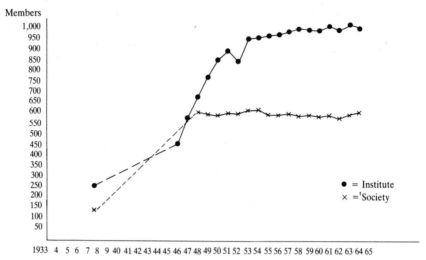

Source: Institute of Housing and Society of Housing Managers annual reports
(Annual figures for the period 1939–46 are missing)
Figure 8.1
Membership of the Society of Housing Managers and the Institute of Housing 1933–1965
(Figures are incomplete because not all records have been retrieved.)

The Council of the Institute had by now gained one woman member "Miss Schofield first joined the Executive Committee, as the governing body was then named, in 1939 and served until 1944. Elected again in 1948 she has served continuously since. As the only woman member until 1950 her contribution on questions of policy, particularly with regard to training and examination was especially valuable".[6] Miss Osborne (Bridgewater) replaced her as the one woman member of Council.

The Society
The admission of men
Women were eligible to join the Institute but within the all female Society the question of whether to admit men aroused much discussion. In fact the question had been raised by the men themselves before the war and by members even during the war. Thus in 1943 a reader wrote "I should like to compare notes with other members who will have been thinking over the suggestion put forward at the A.G.M. about the admission of men to our Society. . . ."[7] In the next issue a rather aggressive writer who called himself a 'mere male' outlined the difficulties which the Society would face in continuing its present policy "What are these qualifications which make women exclusively fitted for housing management about which we hear so much? Will you be able to persuade the Ministry of Health to exclude men from the national post war scheme for housing, whilst you are at the same time protesting against sex discrimination and claiming equality? . . . If the Society

does not take advantage of the progressive lead given it by Octavia Hill, it will, I fear, fall into the same error as the protagonists of Scottish educational standards – so busy talking about how superior their standards are that other organisations will overtake them."[8]

As the post war expansion of housing began, this became of real concern to a number of members of the Society. "There we were with the post war boom in housing – these housing estates being built all over the country and this tremendous need for proper housing management, and yet we – with what we said was such a marvellous training scheme and all our wonderful traditions – we were limiting it to women."

The issue had to be fought out, however, at a number of Annual General Meetings since many, especially the older women, had grave doubts. "Three times at A.G.M.s the vote went in favour of letting men in but not by a big enough majority. I remember Miss . . . pleading with tears in her eyes 'if you let men in, they'll take all the best jobs, they'll be Directors of Housing, you'll be the rent collectors'." "Someone is supposed to have said 'they will take the bread out of our mouths.' I think people were nervous about that, and as it turns out they had something, didn't they?"

"As far as I remember it was mainly the younger people who wanted men to be admitted and the older people who were all agin it. And you couldn't blame them because they'd had to fight, tooth and nail, for recognition and I think they probably foresaw the way we should be taken over by the men. . . ."

Many of the younger members regarded the whole debate as "a lot of nonsense. I mean this I think was us in our most absurd light. I couldn't see the validity of the arguments at all for not admitting men." The split in opinion between older and younger members was not universal, however – the motion to admit men which was eventually successful in 1948 was proposed by Miss Upcott – one of those who had worked with Octavia Hill. The name was therefore changed to the 'Society of Housing Managers (Incorporated)' (S.H.M.). Although men were thus eventually admitted, few joined. Some of the interviewees felt that the five year delay in granting admission to men was a critical factor in the Society's failure to benefit sufficiently from the post war expansion in housing employment.

Principles of housing management
The Society continued to give evidence to official bodies and to press for acceptance of enlightened estate management. However, its members saw the need to adapt their views to post war conditions. The 1954 A.G.M. included a 'full and frank' discussion on the present day principles and practice of housing management. These principles included many points which are being stressed twenty five years later, such as "to encourage initiative on the part of tenants, stimulate pride in the estates and a community spirit".[9] Despite the continued enthusiasm of its members, however, there were worries. In 1958 the report stated "In the face of keen competition from industry and other professions, however, the Society's major problem is still to find enough

students of suitable quality to maintain stability and growth."[10] Concern about recruitment continued for the rest of the Society's life.

The Society's efforts to gain widespread recognition of their views on housing management were encouraged by an invitation to submit evidence to the housing sub-committee of the Central Housing Advisory Committee, enquiring into "The present arrangements for the management of the housing estates of local authorities and in particular the functions of housing managers". This was the first official committee to look at housing management since the 1938 committee and it reported in 1959 in *Councils and their Houses*. In its memorandum the Society stressed the shortage of trained staff, the importance of using them to the best advantage and the need for wider recognition of the value of good management.

In the next year the Society commented "Those who have learnt to control their hopes while awaiting official recommendations will not be too disappointed by the cautious note of some sections of the Report. It is much that the principles which the Society has always upheld are now so widely recognised in the housing world; disagreement probably centres upon the degree of compromise which is necessary in specific circumstances." Disappointment could have centred round two main items. The report failed to give wholehearted support to unified housing management and it failed to give any assistance to training. It was half hearted on the unification of functions. "We recognise, however, the manifest advantages of bringing the various functions of management under a single department. At the same time, we are aware that there are authorities who have achieved efficient and well coordinated management without carrying out complete unification."[11]

The Society had been active in providing various training schemes and the report made the usual kind of approving noises. But no legislative or financial backing was given to training for housing work. The committee said "Efficient management of housing estates of the size and value of those now owned by local authorities cannot be achieved without trained and qualified staff. . . . The professional bodies, however, which provide an examination qualification for housing managers report a shortage of candidates. This should be a matter of great concern to local authorities since it must in time have very serious effects upon the management of their estates."[12] Recommendations to local government included the provision of comprehensive training schemes for 'professional' trainees and consideration of an examination for experienced staff who did not want to take the full professional examination.

The move towards amalgamation

Effort to improve relationships between the two 'professional' bodies had been going on for some time. The Institute's Annual Report for 1954–5 records "Members will be aware that the principle of collaboration with the Society of Housing Managers has become firmly established in recent years, although, so far, it has been limited to discussions on grading and salaries. In an endeavour to strengthen the bond which now exists an approach was made to the Society. . . agreement has been reached on a proposal to set up a Joint

Standing Committee in the first instance for a trial period of one year."[13] The Standing Joint Committee continued. Also the practice of inviting members of the Society to branch meetings and vice versa increased.

The next joint move was on qualifications. The Rt. Hon. Henry Brooke, Minister of Housing and Local Government, addressed the Society's conference in 1960 and "emphasised the points made in *Councils and their Houses* on the responsibilities of housing managers and the need for adequately trained staff". "His concern that consideration should be given to introducing a unified professional qualification has led to consultations between the Society, the Royal Institution of Chartered Surveyors and the Institute of Housing."[14] Discussions began between the Institute and the Society on the possibility of establishing a common examination. . . . By 1961 there was agreement of both bodies to inaugurate a Housing Management Joint Examinations Board to operate from January 1962.

In fact the unification of the examinations was already being succeeded as an issue by the unification of the two organisations. At the Society's A.G.M. in October 1962 it was reported that the Standing Joint Committee had been considering "in what way the new professional organisation should be constituted". "The Society's representatives on the Standing Joint Committee have greatly appreciated the courtesy and spirit of cooperation shown by the Institute members. We have learnt a great deal about each other and many misapprehensions and misunderstandings have been removed." A resolution was carried unanimously "That in view of the present state of the negotiations between the Society and the Institute of Housing on the possibility of forming a new unified professional organisation for those engaged in housing management, Council be authorised to continue the discussions and report further."[15] The Institute agreed to continue negotiations on this.[16]

The reasons behind the move towards unification

In considering this question we must consider three parties – the Institute, the Society and the M.H.L.G. Written records are somewhat sparse and also give only the 'public' reasons. For other material one must rely on the statements of those who took part in the negotiations allowing for personal views. Let us therefore consider the various parties in this transaction.

The Institute. In the report mentioned previously the Institute lists the advantages expected from amalgamation as:
– one voice for the profession which would be more effective for government departments
– an improved Journal
– more adequate headquarters staff
– stronger finances
– a fuller service to members
– a possible future charter for the profession.[17] (A Charter of Incorporation is only granted to a body which can prove that it is unique in its occupational field. Application was subsequently made and, although not granted, still remains an ambition.)

Institute interviewees stressed the evident need to have one voice for the profession and that the new body would be bigger and more powerful.

The Institute had therefore quite a lot to gain. Its membership, after the rapid post war rise, had levelled off; there were obvious advantages in being the one body in the field and not having to compete with the Society, which, despite its smaller numbers, still retained a great amount of prestige.

The Society committee members saw the Institute as potentially having a lot to gain. "The Institute, for their side, looked on us rather as a thorn in the flesh because you see we had two lots of conferences, two lots of journals, etc. and the councillors were getting completely bewildered . . . and it weakened their position you see – they weren't the only body." A particular point mentioned by the Institute interviewees was that a weakness was obviously exposed when the two professional bodies gave conflicting evidence to official enquiries – as had happened before arrangements for cooperation were introduced. As the body with the larger membership the Institute had perhaps less to fear from amalgamation. There were however some objections within the Institute.

Interviewees from the Institute felt that these arose from two sources. The first was the view that the 'ladies from the Society' were dogmatic in adherence to the 'pure Octavia Hill system' (i.e. qualified staff in charge of small groups of properties) which they did not feel suitable for large modern organisations. The second was the fact that when two organisations exist in this way for some years their members may have somewhat distorted ideas about each other. "There were people on both sides who took the most ridiculous attitudes for years. Women who felt that men hadn't the right personal qualities for housing management. Men who thought 'these are a lot of sloppy women who get all sentimental about housing'."

The Society. The Society interviewees felt that the major reason for unification was that it now seemed appropriate to have two separate bodies dealing with housing. The decision in 1948 to admit men to membership meant that there was no longer the same rationale for a separate organisation. And the Society had for some time been concerned about recruitment and finance.

"We weren't getting more members . . . our total membership 350 . . . 15 students coming in the year . . . it's just ludicrous if you are thinking of the country as a whole . . . getting the benefits of what we thought we'd got to a wider field."

"I think I felt we had got to expand in numbers if we weren't just to flicker out."

"Well I think after the joint exam there seemed very little reason why not – we had the same qualification."

"It seemed a bit silly to have two different organisations in the same field and we felt that we could have a better organisation with the two joining together."

The experience of working together on the Standing Joint Committee had been important in overcoming initial reservations. "We got to know each other . . . there were some misconceptions on both sides." However a number of interviewees felt that the negotiating body had not been an entirely accurate representation of the Institute. "They were pretty good people and what we didn't realise was how far advanced they were in their thinking from the rank and file." The Institute interviewees cast some light on this by explaining that, because the Institute had for so many years admitted members without qualifications, it was a far less homogenous body than the Society, which had from the beginning set educational standards and closely supervised the training of its students. Society members realised that these high standards aroused mixed feelings at the Institute. "They were frightened of us. The majority of our members were better trained than the majority of their members – and they were frightened . . . this came out in discussion."

Thus within the Society there were some doubts about the unification. Looking back it seems perhaps strange that issues of the employment of women did not seem to appear very prominently in the discussion. Publicly expressed qualms were much more about the proposal to abandon the specific commitment in the Articles to the "practice of housing management in the Octavia Hill tradition". One member wrote "The principles of housing management are still as practical today as they were 50 years ago when practiced by Octavia Hill and any thought of omitting these from our constitution causes me both dismay and bewilderment."[18] Mrs Barclay, one of the older members, replied "Her reaction to the amalgamation of our society with another and larger body which has not in the past visualised property management as equally a technical profession and one requiring social work training was my first reaction too. That was some years ago and I am sure Miss Breakwell shares with me and all members of our Society the utmost confidence in our officers who are labouring so to achieve this difficult amalgamation without sacrificing the ideals for which we stand."[19]

Despite the good reasons for unification many, even of the committee members, had their doubts. "I had a feeling they would swamp us eventually – it came more quickly than I expected," "people still had their misgivings about the Institute", "pretty superficial in their attitudes and pretty lacking in any academic training. There were many for example who'd come in on this ex-forces exam thing, and I think we suspected, and afterwards found out that it was, you know, as easy as falling off a log."

However it was felt on the whole that it was 'old fashioned' to feel that women any longer had the need for a separate predominantly female society, that women could now make their way on their own merits and that the Institute had by now adopted attitudes towards housing management which were closer to those of the Society. We will see in the next chapter how women fared within the Institute after unification.

Central government. The role of central government in recommending a unified qualification has already been described. The majority of interviewees both from the Society and the Institute also believed that there was pressure from the Ministry to unify the professional institutions, though this is not documented. Interviewees made statements such as "The first thing that happened was the Ministry . . . they found it difficult to have these two bodies. . . ." "I believe the Ministry said that it would be better if we got together . . .

politely . . . perhaps through informal contacts."

As written records are not yet open to investigation these views can only be recorded without comment.

Progress towards unification

The Standing Joint Committee produced their *Report on Unification* in May 1963. This repeated the arguments for unification but acknowledged the difficulty "It would be idle to pretend that with bodies originally incorporated or founded in 1930 and 1931, there have been no differences in professional outlook over the years."[20]

In fact, as we have seen, there were reservations on both sides and the Standing Joint Committee were in a position, typical of negotiators,[21] of "fighting two battles . . . you were negotiating with the enemy so to speak and fighting a rearguard action with your own troops". (Institute interviewee.) Both sides were anxious that the bulk of their membership should be carried along with them and that a further split should not result. This aim seems largely to have been achieved, though there is no record of a specific check of any 'fall out' of membership on unification. Appropriate agreement was reached in the Annual General Meetings of both bodies and the new Institute of Housing Managers came into being in April 1965. The Society and the Institute were dissolved.

Thus nearly 50 years of having a separate women's organisation in housing management came to an end. It is difficult to assess the overall influence of the Society but in many ways it seems to have had a standing out of proportion to its small numbers, largely because of the quality of its membership. It had consistently emphasised in its work, submissions to official bodies, and publicity the importance of the proper management of all rented housing. Many members felt, by the time of the amalgamation, that much of this battle had been won. At least the Institute of Housing had moved nearer to a similar position. However as a profession housing management was still weak. This meant that the status of those who managed and had practical experience of housing was low in relation to that of those who designed it. In practical terms this meant that a housing manager objecting to an architect's plans would often be overruled. There were those who felt, and still feel, that some of the worst excesses of post war public building would have been avoided if those who were responsible for managing it had had a stronger voice. Whether or not the existence of a separate Society had added to this weakness the unification of the two organisations was probably necessary in order to get a better hearing for these views.

The Society's very specific contribution, particularly in its early years, had been to fight for the employment of women in housing. It had actively sought to recruit women to this work. Even after 1948, when the admission of men must have modified this role, younger women were able to see women of standing and authority in the field of housing management and in their professional body.

The next chapter will show how women fared in the new organisation and in the field of employment after unification.

References
1. Society of Women Housing Managers. *Bulletin*, January 1941, p. 1.
2. J. Burnett. *Social History of Housing*, David and Charles, 1978, pp. 213–71.
3. Society of Women Housing Managers. *Minutes of Council*, July 1944.
4. Institute of Housing. *Annual Report*, 1945–46.
5. I.O.H. *Annual Report*, 1946–47.
6. I.O.H. *Annual Report*, 1955–56.
7. C. L. Cook. Letter to Society of Women Housing Managers, *Bulletin,* January 1944, p. 10.
8. 'A Mere Male'. S.W.H.M. *Bulletin*, June 1944, p. 12.
9. S.H.M. *Annual Report*, 1954–55, p. 3.
10. S.H.M. *Annual Report*, 1957–58, p. 1.
11. Central Housing Advisory Committee. *Councils and Their Houses*, H.M.S.O., 1959, p. 8.
12. *Ibid.*, paragraph 136, p. 30.
13. S.H.M. *Annual Report*, 1954–5.
14. S.H.M. *Annual Report*, 1959–60, p. 1.
15. S.H.M. *Annual Report*, 1962–63, p. 2.
16. I.O.H. *Annual Report*, 1961–62.
17. *Ibid.*
18. B. B. Breakwell. Letter, S.H.M. *Quarterly Journal*, January 1963, p. 14.
19. I. T. Barclay. Letter, S.H.M. *Quarterly Journal*, July 1963, p. 17.
20. The Institute of Housing and the Society of Housing Managers Standing Joint Committee *Report on Unification*, May 1963, p. 4.
21. J. Z. Rubin and B. R. Brown. *The Social Psychology of Bargaining and Negotiation*, Academic Press, London 1975, p. 13.

CHAPTER 9

Women in the Housing Service 1965–1977

Introduction

The unification of the two professional associations in 1965 was followed by a reduction in the proportion of qualified members who were women and it seems that by 1977 fewer women occupied senior posts in housing organisations. Evidence will be presented about what happened during this period. We start with the views of the committee which dealt with the unification of the two associations. In the next part of the chapter evidence is given of the small role which women played both as Council members and in employment. This might not have mattered had the proportion of women reaching senior posts in housing gone up or even remained stable but it seemed to fall, most notably in housing associations. The reasons for the poor achievement of women are complex. It is suggested that the lack of a single sex professional association was only one factor.

Committee members' views on changes in the Institute after unification

Most Society interviewees felt that, given the circumstances, the unification had been inevitable. Nevertheless, many felt that some of the original aims had not been achieved. The 'Institute' interviewees were more emphatic about the benefits of unification and did not generally feel that anything had been lost, apart from the disappearance of ex-Society members from the Council. We summarise below views about the gains and losses of unification.

The status of the professional body

Most 'Society' interviewees felt that the aim of gaining a better professional body had not been achieved. It was true that numbers had increased but they felt that it had been 'rather a second rate professional body'. They considered that the possibility of a rise in status had been weakened by the new Institute's 'rump' of unqualified staff and by practices such as allowing student members to remain as such for many years. "I fear that in housing it is going to be a very very long time, if at all, before the profession is respected." Some felt that there had been gains, though not as much as hoped "The new Institute was a much better body than the old Institute". "Housing management is still a Cinderella. We probably made housing management stronger but it is still very small."

The 'Institute' interviewees were more unanimous and more certain about the benefits. "The gain was that we had a single body speaking with a single voice . . . I think that enhances its status with government departments and with other bodies." Most interviewees felt that the standard of training in the new Institute was an improvement on the old. On the other hand, a number of the Society interviewees felt that it still was not as good as it should be. Although some higher standards had been adopted, the level of practical training provided in the Society's training offices had been lost.

Financially, all members were clear that a sensible decision had been taken. It was clearly more economical to run one organisation rather than to duplicate functions.

Social aspects

Nearly all Society interviewees felt there had been a loss of the close sense of association enjoyed by members of the Society – though a number felt that this closeness could degenerate into something slightly smug and clique-ish. "Well we lost the sort of cosy club and the historical links with Octavia Hill. . . ."

"Loss of the clubby atmosphere of the Society – a wonderful bunch of people."

"I mean the A.G.M. used to be enormous fun – meeting people – most of us have made life long friends of people we'd worked with . . . – a wonderful atmosphere . . . on the same wavelength. . . ."

Most, however, felt there had been some gain in opening out the slightly 'smug' atmosphere that had sometimes prevailed in the Society. Also, they were aware of its somewhat upper middle class nature, though many pointed out that this was inevitable at a time when the majority of women educated enough to meet the entrance requirements, and having the resources to carry them through the training period, were likely to come from upper middle class backgrounds. The new generation coming in after the war and later were felt, in any case, to have a less upper class bias. There were no comments from 'Institute' interviewees on these aspects.

Opportunities for women

Most interviewees, both from the Society and the Institute, felt that the participation of women in the new Institute had been much less than was hoped for. This is a matter which we will explore in more detail later. But some ex-Society members felt that one of the aims of amalgamation, the opening up of more offices, especially in local government, to women, had to some extent been achieved. "Basically, in the old days the Society was Housing Association orientated – it used to madden me in my local government days. I wanted to see us capturing local government."

In the next sections of this chapter the available statistics will be examined to see what light they cast on these comments, firstly in relation to membership of the Council of the Institute and then in relation to different types of employment. Finally some of the factors affecting the employment of qualified women in housing will be considered.

Membership of the Council of the Institute 1965–77

On the Council of the new Institute retiring members were only ineligible for re-election if they had served for six years continuously. This differed from the Society which had a provision that if the retiring member had served for 18 months or more he or she was ineligible for one year following. Provision was made to ensure that each Branch was represented. As a temporary measure, because of the unification of the two bodies, there was a mechanism to ensure that a minimum of 25 per cent of former members of each of the former bodies should be included on the Council for an initial period of three years.

Figure 9.1 shows the membership of the Council of the new Institute from 1965 to 1980. It demonstrates very clearly that, once the guaranteed three year period for representation of ex-Society members was over, the number of women on the new Institute's Council began to fall. Once the decline in numbers began it was very rapid indeed and the lowest point came from 1972 to 1974 when there was only one woman member of Council – a position which was a return to the situation of the old male dominated Institute which for year after year had one woman member. In the words of one committee member "The Society sank without trace". What was the reason for this complete crumbling away of the Society's representation? It is clear that one argument which is often advanced, that women are unwilling to take office, can hardly apply. For thirty years women had been running their own Society and filling all the positions of honorary officers. Even if some of the members were growing older this would not by itself have caused such a sudden difference. This question was discussed with interviewees and a number of answers were common, though there was considerable difference of emphasis.

Reasons for the lack of women Council members

The process of election

The actual mechanics of election without proportional representation work against any minority and Society interviewees were aware of this.

"I think it was partly that those of us who put up were not in any way known to the rank and file member. I think also that the reputation we had among Institute people was of a lot of old fuddy duddies who didn't know anything about anything and therefore weren't worth voting for. One got an awful lot of jibes about Octavia Hill . . . about ladies going round with ink bottles strapped to their waist and so forth. . . ."

The effect of electoral arrangements was accentuated by the provision for branch representation. Most ex-Society members were not well known in the branches and in each branch they would be a small minority. "People vote for those whom they know" and it was only in a few exceptional cases that women ex-Society members were well enough known to gain election. In addition, where there was a concentration of better known members in the London area, there was also much more competition for places.

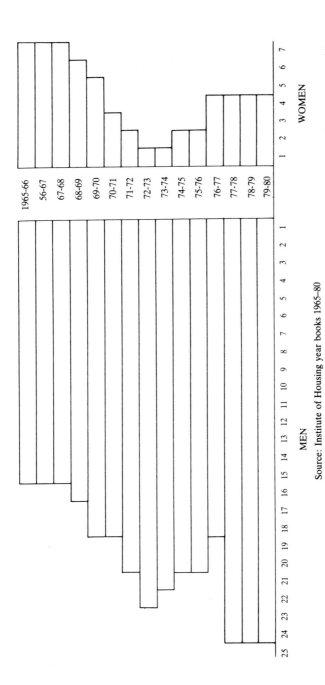

Figure 9.1
Men and women members of Institute of Housing Council 1965–1980

Source: Institute of Housing year books 1965–80

Two interviewees felt that there had been a rather more deliberate attempt to eliminate the influence of the Society, "I was discussing something with an Institute member who said '. . . you did not think about it when we amalgamated, that we would be two to one and we'd get everybody on'. Well I mean, we had thought about it and that wasn't our idea at all, we thought that we'd vote for people on their merits."

It is only fair to say, however, that most members did not share this view of a deliberate campaign to eliminate ex-Society representation. The Institute interviewees all expressed regret about the loss of this representation. They felt that Institute members had always favoured the election of people at the top of the profession, who had the 'big' jobs and as one said "this inevitably did not take cognisance of the fact that these admirable ladies were not elected – I and other colleagues regretted that they dropped out". "It was a tragedy that these very talented people did not remain on Council."

Differing attitudes to service on the governing body

There was a fairly common view among Society interviewees that the nature of the governing body and attitudes to serving on it had both changed.

". . . and of course they are rather formal, they do rather indulge in mayors and formal lunches and speeches and things which isn't our style of thing at all . . . much more status, wearing chains and things . . . I think men are like that, like that sort of thing . . . I don't think women do to the same extent and found it difficult to play up to that sort of thing."

"The Institute Council was a whole weekday . . . women don't as easily as men abandon the office for the whole day."

"I don't like generalising but on the whole men tend to be more ambitious, they rather like being able to say 'I'm a member of the Council'."

"In the Society . . . when you'd been on Council say for two periods of three years and it was Friday nights, Saturdays all day and Sundays till lunchtime, you were thankful when your time came and you couldn't be elected. In the Institute they struggled to get on and once on they never thought of getting off."

'Society' interviewees commented that the provision for a 'retirement' of one year after six years on Council had often been circumvented by use of the provision of places on Council for the Immediate Past President and ex-officio members. There was not the same positive attitude to encouraging more junior members.

"On the whole, the Institute, they tend to elect to Council people who are in the really big jobs."

"The Society had more junior people on Council."

"There was a tradition that the senior members of the Society kept an eye out the whole time for young people coming up and you always saw on your voting list some of the 'old guard' and some new names so there was a constant stream of younger people going through Council . . . and they were always bringing on new people."

In addition, they felt that, once the sense of 'belonging' and obligation to their own Society had gone, women were less motivated to add extra committees to their work and were definitely, on the whole, much less likely to be competitive about it.

"Well, I don't think that we're, on the whole, all that interested in that kind of thing really. If you take away the 'club atmosphere' which was very enjoyable . . . I don't think that most of us are frightfully keen on meetings and extra things."

"And also, on the whole, we're not so pushing, and don't mind whether we're on committees or not. . . ."

Institute interviewees did not seem to be aware of these differences in style.

Lack of participation generally

Most interviewees agreed that there had been a lack of participation of ex-Society members at branch level which had exacerbated the fact that they were not generally so well known. This was often linked with a difference in attitudes.

"Well the attitude of the two was so different. I mean the Institute, they gave more importance to projecting their image than to maintaining high standards. (That's my opinion, I may be wrong.) And the speakers who spoke on behalf of the Institute, they were long winded, they were wordy, they just wanted to hear their own voices . . . I just dropped out."

". . . and then I think when we began to come to the surface again and attended some of the lectures and the meetings . . . talks and discussions were of such poor quality, quite honestly, that I personally felt it was a waste of time. . . ."

In a minority, women felt outnumbered "rather than stay and battle with them on their own terms we shrugged and turned away. . . ."

"I was the only ex-Society and Housing Association member and I felt utterly miserable."

"I think they (women) tend to just say . . . do their own work in the office as well as they can and feel that it's a bit hopeless. Perhaps they give up too easily, I don't know."

This was for some members linked with the loss of the 'clubby' atmosphere mentioned in the earlier part of the chapter. The members of the new Institute no longer shared a common outlook and type of training; in these circumstances the women ex-Society members, who were in a minority anyway, felt a lack of 'belonging' and only the most determined continued active participation. As members participating dropped the feeling of being in a minority would increase and therefore reinforce itself.

A certain amount of difference in views of housing management itself was also important. The Society had emphasised the 'Octavia Hill tradition', the importance of the social aspects of housing and the individual tenant. The Institute had always been dominated by housing departments. In the early 1960s a view of housing management which proclaimed that it was a 'business like any other business' seemed to be becoming increasingly popular. Institute interviewees stressed the difference in views of what housing work should be like and the fact that Society members did not seem so interested in the development of the comprehensive housing service.

An overview

This disappearance of the 'Society' influence and membership after 1965 can be related to the general literature about group interaction as well as to the specific work on women's groups.

The general literature tells us that when any two groups of people who have developed a separate 'culture' are brought together there is bound to be some hostility and suspicion.[1] Argyle's observation that "Groups develop norms of behaviour, which can be regarded as a kind of culture in miniature. . . . Anyone who fails to conform is placed under pressure to do so, and if he does not is rejected"[2] appeals to common experience as well as to experimental evidence. The Institute and the Society had different 'norms' – since the Society members were in the minority they would be expected to conform. This was likely to be even more marked because men are conditioned to regard themselves as the 'norm'.

The literature of the Women's Liberation movement argues that in the present cultural circumstances, in any mixed sex organisation men take over the reins of power and the dominating role. "Women in virtually every group in the United States, Canada, and Europe soon discovered that when men were present, the traditional sex roles reasserted themselves regardless of the good intentions of the participants. Men inevitably dominated the discussions."[3] Thus, while the Society of Housing Managers was well able to produce its own Council and leaders as a predominantly single sex organisation, once the mixed sex organisation came into being "traditional sex roles reasserted themselves".

The extracts from the interviews have illustrated that the Society and the Institute had very different styles of organisation and again this has been shown to be significant – that when women do organise they do it in a different way from men. A historical study of a women's organisation in the U.S.A. said: "The Association was not exactly public . . . rather, the Association relied on informal but expansive social ties and a voluntary network of like minded individuals . . . social organisations of this nature are particularly receptive to female participation."[4] The Society's way of organising itself and greater informality had suited its women members; after amalgamation, however, meetings and procedures tended to revert to the patterns of the old Institute. The 'submerging' of the Society's membership and culture was thus only too easily explicable – one committee member who had perhaps had more experience of 'power politics' than most felt that it was entirely foreseeable.

The most recent years have seen a small apparent revival with the representation of women on Council returning to two in 1975 and to four in

1977, which year saw the election of a woman president. This might seem to indicate an improvement in the position of women within the Institute. A generation of younger members is growing up with much less of a separate 'culture' and it will be interesting to watch developments over the next few years. However, we have so far only discussed the position of women in the Institute's Council. It would be illogical to expect much representation of women if they were not represented in the membership. So the overall position of women members of the Institute between 1965 and 1977 must now be examined.

Changes in the distribution of qualified staff 1965–77

Between 1965 and 1977 the total membership of the Institute rose from just over 2,000 to nearly 4,000. Table 9.1, however, shows that the proportion of *qualified* members who were women had fallen from 26 per cent in 1965 to 17 per cent in 1977 and the overall figure of 21 per cent was only maintained because the proportion of students who were women had risen from 15 per cent in 1965 to 24 per cent in 1977.

Table 9.1

Men and women members of Institute of Housing 1965 and 1977

		1965			1977		
		Men	Women	Total	Men	Women	Total
Members*		902	310	1,212	1,314	262	1,576
	%	74%	26%		83%	17%	
Students		803	139	942	1,728	535	2,263
	%	85%	15%		76%	24%	
All members		1,705	449	2,154	3,042	797	3,839
	%	79%	21%		79%	21%	

* Including members, Fellows and licentiates. Excluding retired and overseas members.
Source: Institute of Housing Year Books, analysis of employed members.

The fall in the percentage of qualified members who were women has considerable significance. Students in the Institute cannot vote and have very little influence on the way in which the organisation is run. The 'real' membership is the qualified membership who are entitled to vote in elections and it is here that women lost out significantly in the period after unification. The difference can also be seen strikingly in the actual numbers. There were fewer qualified women members in employment in 1977 (262) than there had been in 1965 (310).

On the other hand there were 1,314 qualified male members in 1977 compared with 967 Institute members in 1954 and 261 in 1936. Moreover, the constitution of the new Institute gave a greater proportion of the membership of the Council to Fellows (in effect people holding senior positions) than had been the case in the Society. At the time of the amalgamation there had been

199 male and 59 female Fellows in employment. By 1977 this had changed to 235 male Fellows and only 39 female Fellows in employment. This is one of the differences which gives a clue to the change in status of the women in the Institute as well as in the numerical balance. Although the evidence is not conclusive this change becomes more evident when we break down the figures by place of employment – departments, housing associations and 'other employers' – as in Table 9.2.

Table 9.2

Proportions of men and women Institute members by employer: 1965 and 1977

	1965		1977	
	Men	Women	Men	Women
Departments %	85	15	87	13
Housing Associations %	17	83	69	31
Other employers %	55	45	74	26
Total %	74	26	83	17

Source: Institute of Housing Year Books, analysis of employed members.

Housing departments

Table 9.2 shows a slight decline in the position of women members in employment with local authority housing departments. 13 per cent of members employed in local authorities in 1977 were women as opposed to 15 per cent in 1965. Within local authority types there was only a small amount of variation. There were slightly more women members in London than in the District Councils but in both cases the percentage who were women had declined by two or three per cent between 1965 and 1977.

Since London local government reorganisation had taken place by 1965 it is possible to look in more detail at the record of individual Boroughs over time. In 1968 there were 12 London Boroughs listed with no women members or students. In 1977 there were only five offices without any women members or students. Of these City of London, Barking, Croydon and Bexley had been 'all male' offices in 1965. The addition was Hounslow which had one woman student in 1968 but no women members in 1977. On the other hand Haringey, Newham, Sutton and Wandsworth had acquired women members and students and Barnet, Harrow and Sutton had acquired women students only. There is thus some indication that one of the aims of the Society of Housing Managers, the 'opening up' of more municipal employment to women, had been achieved. However, one must bear in mind that the overall percentage of women members in employment with London Boroughs had fallen.

Though more offices might be open to women students this did not necessarily mean that it was as easy for women to gain promotion. Some indication of this can be gained by looking at heads of departments and deputy and assistant directors listed as members. In 1965 of 31 Boroughs with heads of departments listed in Institute membership only two (6 per cent) had women heads of departments. There were however ten (32 per cent) which had women deputies. In 1977 28 Boroughs had listed members as heads of departments. Of these four (14 per cent) were women. On the other hand 22 Boroughs had listed deputy or assistant directors, of which only one (4 per cent) was a woman. This would not seem to augur well for the proportion of women in the next generation of heads of departments. Of the four women heads of departments in 1977 only one had not been a head or a deputy in 1968. By 1979 only three remained.

Housing associations

In 1965 Housing Associations had a relatively high proportion of women members (83 per cent) to men (17 per cent). By 1977 the position was reversed, with men forming 69 per cent and women forming 31 per cent of the qualified members in employment. In fact the reversal in terms of the grade of jobs was probably even greater than this. An examination of the posts listed in terms of grade of job held shows that in 1977 60 of the men employed in Housing Associations held the position of Secretary, Housing Manager or Director, while only 22 women held such posts. In 1965 there were 19 women members listed as Secretary, Director or Housing Manager but only eight men with such posts. So that whereas in 1965 70 per cent of staff listed in the more senior jobs were women in 1977 this had dropped to 27 per cent. Clearly the changes over this period of time are subject to all kinds of influences and we will discuss some of these later. And not all senior officers of housing associations, by any means, are Institute members. Even so there seems to be confirmation of the view that although a higher proportion of qualified women worked in housing associations even here they were no longer getting the top jobs.

'Other employers'

As Table 9.2 shows even the 'other employers' who had a fairly even split (55 per cent men and 45 per cent women) in 1965 had also increased their proportion of men by 1971 (74 per cent men to 26 per cent women). The 'other employers' include a variety of organisations from other public authorities to private owners and members working as lecturers or consultants.

The general inference seems to be therefore that women lost out most heavily in those areas (housing associations and 'other bodies') where they and the Society were strongest before 1965. Before going on to discuss the factors affecting this, however, one fundamental question must be asked. Was the reason for the reduction in the number of women members in employment simply the fact that they failed to sit for, or pass the examinations?

The output of qualified staff

The number of students rose considerably after unification. Table 9.3 shows the distribution of men and women students passing the Final examination

Table 9.3

Institute of housing students qualifying 1965–1977

	Men	Women	Total	Women as % of total
1965	25	12	37	32
1966	15	5	20	25
1967	25	9	34	26
1968	35	8	43	19
1969	42	13	55	24
1970	79	14	93	15
1971	148	22	170	13
1972	24	4	28	14
1973	68	22	90	24
1974	101	33	134	25
1975	113	31	144	22
1976	133	37	170	22
1977	166	84	250	34
1978	182	77	259	30

Source: Institute of Housing Annual Reports and Journals. 1965–1978.

after 1965. In that year 32 per cent of students qualifying were women. This proportion dropped consistently after amalgamation until it reached its lowest point of 13 per cent in 1971. After that point it slowly rose until it reached 34 per cent in 1977. It is interesting to see that this 'dip' in the number of women corresponded (to some extent) with the dip in the number of women on the Council. This correlation should not, however, argue for causation. It is probably more likely that both proportions were reacting to external factors which we will discuss later. It is also important to note the effect of increased overall numbers. Thus 32 per cent of the total only represented 12 women in 1965; 34 per cent represented 84 women in 1977. The number of women qualifying in 1977 and 1978 represented a much sharper increase than the preceding years. It will be most interesting to see whether this increase is sustained.

Thus after an initial decline the number of women students has been maintained relatively well compared with that of women at other levels. Two factors may be significant here. The first is that, as has already been pointed out, after unification at least some offices which had all male Institute membership in the past did take in women students. The second likely factor is that there has been an increasing interest in recruitment of graduates to housing and graduates were available to enter these jobs. Most of the women recruited by S.W.H.M. had been graduates or at least had some further education. But more of the Institute's recruits had come from people already employed in housing departments or local authorities. Because of the nature of most of these departments it is likely that most of those recruits would be men. The increasing tendency to advertise trainee posts nationally and to recruit graduates, and the increased willingness of some departments to recruit women are therefore probably the most important factors increasing the proportion of women students since 1973. It is also possible that the Equal Opportunities legislation has had an influence here, since it is easier to identify discrimination in the recruitment of graduates, who have a more common level of attainment, than with mature staff.

It is clear, however, that at all times the proportion of women qualifying was considerably higher than the proportion of women members of the Institute of Housing and of women reaching high office in housing. Also there was a decline in both numbers around 1971–74 and some revival since. Why should this be?

Reasons for the changes in the position of women members
Change in the careers of women qualifying

The effect of a marriage, and particularly a break for childbearing, on women's careers is well documented[5]. But if this is a constant factor it would not explain a change in the employment of women in housing over a period of time. However, it seems probable, though difficult to document precisely, that the 'core' members of the Society of Housing Managers contained a large proportion of women who were unmarried, widowed or childless and who could thus pursue their careers with a little less complication (though a proportion of them, like so many women, might have elderly relatives to care for). Interviewees confirmed this fact. The generation of women trained after the war, if it followed the general pattern, probably had a larger proportion who both married and had children.[6] Previous studies have shown that, apart from the exceptional women who continue to work with little break, childbearing takes women out of the labour market just at the time when men are gaining vital promotion.[7] The career patterns of successful men in housing are often similar to those of successful civil servants with the difference that instead of moving from one department to another they move from one employing organisation to another.[8] If women do return to housing employment after having children (and because no research has been done on this we cannot say categorically how many do) they have often missed out on this vital stage of gaining middle management experience; they may also be less mobile and unable to take advantage of promotion opportunities through movements to other authorities.

It is worth noting that over half of the women interviewed, though they were people who had reached some eminence in housing, had been 'held' at some stage in their career by family responsibilities, either children or elderly or ill parents.

"If I hadn't had (family responsibilities) I would probably have gone and taken a much bigger job."

Some of the older generation had assumed that having a career ruled out marriage "If you did a job you didn't get married . . . in general we assumed it was a choice."

Thus one of the reasons for the 'relapse' in the number of women Institute members may have been that more of them married and dropped out of membership either permanantly or for a period. There have been no formal schemes to encourage qualified women housing staff to return to work. In fact, an extreme shortage of qualified or experienced staff in the 1960–70 period did mean that some part time qualified staff were encouraged to return to work but this, as in other occupations, was only regarded as an expedient. If full time posts only are available the hours and pressure of housing work are not such as to make it easy for women with young children to work. At the moment, as no finance is available for an adequate survey, it is not possible to say how many qualified women are entirely 'lost' from housing work because of this. Studies in other occupations have pointed out the cost of such 'wastage' and mature staff are particularly needed in housing. However, only a few employers are currently improving conditions for women with children to return to work.

Housing work and the woman's role

Many of the authors who have written on men's and women's careers have commented on the effect of stereotyped notions of men's and women's work. Thus it has been 'acceptable' for women to work in caring occupations or those closely connected with the home, such as nursing, domestic work, teaching, catering and secretarial work. Many more difficulties are raised when women engage in occupations with a 'masculine' and particularly 'outdoor' image like civil engineering, the armed forces or heavy industry. In general this stereotyping is also extended to the management role as such. Management, particularly top management of large organisations, is seen as requiring qualities of mind which are more usually considered to be found in a man than in a woman.[9] Particularly when men are in the majority during the selection process it is easy for women to be passed over for promotion.

Housing management stood from the beginning in a rather ambiguous position with regard to this stereotyping of sex roles. As we have seen, the initial intervention of women in housing work was aided by an emphasis on the 'soft' role of women. For example Kingsley stressed "the necessity for women to take up the work because on it the saving of infant life so much depended".[10] Similarly Shaftesbury "explained how much of the work in its practical detail was specially suited to women, while the legislative must be done by men."[11] Thus the traditional role division was not challenged by the first advocates of women in housing.

Women themselves then and now are often strongly influenced by these stereotypes. Thus Beatrice Webb saw that "there is an increasing number of women to whom a matrimonial career is shut, and who seek a masculine reward for masculine qualities".[12]

Members of the Society were not averse to using the 'soft' image when they felt it necessary. "The Society claimed that because of her sex it was easier for a woman than a man to get on friendly terms with the housewife who was the real manager of the home . . . whilst a male rent collector often waited on the doorstep, a woman manager was asked to step inside and indeed in times of sickness to visit the housewife in her bedroom. . . ."[13]

There were obviously dangers in using these kinds of argument to bolster women's' position in housing work and these are amply illustrated by correspondence in the *Municipal Journal* in the mid 1930's. Ernest France, 'Chairman of the Rent Collectors and Investigators, Manchester' wrote an article entitled "Will new municipal Housing Estates become slums? What efficient and scientific management can do: a job for men, women or both?" In it he argued the case for "good landlordism" but claimed that the women property managers did not have a monopoly of this. "There must be several hundreds of technically qualified officers in the service of local authorities. . . . They have found the right way, and many of them . . . are ready to endorse the methods and principles of the late Octavia Hill."[14] While acknowledging Octavia Hill's pioneer work he went on to point out her opposition to municipal housing and to argue that men had some advantages as opposed to women in doing the job. "It is probably true also that a housewife would more readily accept a suggestion or a reprimand from a man." However he advocated that "estate management is, and must remain, an open-sex occupation" and that the Society and the Institute should unite. This article sparked off a lively correspondence which reveals many of the attitudes on both sides. The women emphasised that the pioneer work had been done by Octavia Hill and that it was by women that the principles of enlightened management had been developed since that date.

"But we do claim that the profession of housing estate management is and will remain one for which women, by reason of character and temperament are specially well adapted and in which, given the requisite training, they are able to do specially valuable work."[15]

"It is on the side of their human relationships with the tenants that women have the greatest natural advantages over men . . . they are by temperament more interested in people for their own sakes. . . ."[16]

Such views provoked a strong reaction from L. W. Mascall, Housing Welfare Officer for Dudley, who went so far as to suggest "that their enthusiasm is liable to blind them to the obvious natural disadvantages they experience by reason of their status in life, apart from official existence. Far from having a pull over a man it is to be found that when a conscientious housing official enters a home where tenancy relations are normal, he straightaway finds himself on common ground.". . . [17] As Jean Thompson said in her letter of reply the "natural disadvantages to women" are obscure unless it just meant that the majority of such women were single, but many young male managers were single also. In this letter Miss Thompson exposed the dilemma the women were in. "I would say that all spheres of work in the public service should be open-sex occupations. If so it would be found that women had a special aptitude for housing estate management, just as men have for example, for certain branches of technical work. In both cases there is no reason why a minority of exceptional people of the other sex should not do useful work if they were fitted for it."[18]

"Such a complete freedom of entry to all branches of the service for both sexes would secure a natural adjustment of interest, the best use of qualifications and the highest level of service for the community. But this is not the case at present. The public service is full of . . . *closed sex* occupations – closed to women."

"No doubt the men who are so anxious to define housing as an open-sex occupation would agree that the principle should be extended to the other branches. Until it is, it must continue to be emphasised that women as such and by virtue of higher education and specialised training have special qualifications for housing management, both in the larger and smaller areas and not only in subordinate positions."[19] Thus the women, just because they were in such a disadvantaged position at a time when many jobs were still closed to them, were forced to use the 'special aptitude' argument which could so easily be turned against them. In the atmosphere of the time it was not easy to query the standard sexual stereotypes though it had become possible to admit that exceptional people of the other sex might possess similar attributes.

However when we read the factual accounts of the practice of housing management by Octavia Hill, Maud Jeffery, Jean Thompson, Irene Barclay and many others we see that the job itself was very different from the 'soft' stereotype. Housing managers who carried out the full range of work as recommended by S.W.H.M. were responsible for collecting their own rents, following up tenants in arrears and doing their own accounts – despite the fact that dealing with money has always had a rather 'masculine' image. Besides this a housing manager was responsible for ordering and some supervision of repairs and increasingly in later years, particularly in associations, for judgements relating to the acquisition of property, its improvement or demolition and plans for rebuilding. The building trade has always remained a predominantly 'masculine' one and indeed attempts of women in recent years to work directly as building labourers has met with particularly marked hostility, though such employment may be common elsewhere in the world. It is relevant to note that in the other major professions connected with building – architecture, planning and surveying, – women have not done well in penetrating the occupational field. Despite the close association of architecture with peoples' homes only five per cent of architects are women and women architects often feel themselves at a disadvantage.[20] Surveyors' women membership is even smaller – less than one per cent in 1976.[21]

It can therefore be seen that in their initial progress in housing management women were moving into a field with a predominantly 'masculine' image. Their success in establishing themselves must partly be due to the fact that there was no established male dominated professional group to keep them out. Once having formed their own professional group they could, as we have seen during the 1930s, actively encourage the recruitment and employment of women in housing. But having gained this position, why did they suffer this relative relapse during the late 60s and 70s? Was this due just to increased marriage rates and the disappearance of the predominantly womens' organisation or were other factors at work?

Growth in the size of housing organisations

It is likely that at least one other significant factor was emerging in the 1960s. This period was one both of growth in the housing stock and in the powers of housing departments, – with the idea of the comprehensive housing service taking root. Similarly housing associations, from being on the whole small organisations with limited charitable funds, became instead larger organisations with considerable development programmes funded to a great extent by central government money. London government reorganisation in 1965 and general local government reorganisation in 1974 produced much larger housing organisations with much more powerful and demanding top management jobs. At the same time the hugely increased salaries made them much more attractive to men. Previous work on factors affecting womens' careers has shown that sexual stereotyping works against women being awarded such top management jobs.[22] In many cases where several authorities were merged during reorganisation it was the existing male member of staff who became the Director and the existing female chief officer who became Assistant Director or Deputy Housing Manager. The women who survived local government reorganisation as heads of housing department were either very lucky or very gifted.

Walton studied the same process in detail within the social work profession.[23] Social work had started off as being a predominantly female occupation but with increasing scope and a rise in salaries more men were recruited and "men were already occupying a disproportionate number of senior positions in the 1950s and 1960s and it seems the fate of social work that it will fall under the domination of men". Walton saw the worsening position of women in social work as resulting from several mutually supportive tendencies. "First, local government's male domination at senior levels, and lay committee's identification of managerial skills with men, might give a bias towards the male candidates to restore the male club into which women children's officers had been an uncomfortable intrusion at times". The special place which women had had on children's committees would tend to disappear and the chairmanship of the social services committee would become a key political appointment. Second, many of the women children's officers had been in post for many years . . . and may have been approaching retirement; . . . Third, at the levels below chief officer there was already a disproportionate weighting of men in senior positions. Fourth, these highly paid posts were extremely attractive to men." . . .[24]

It is likely that many similar processes were operating in housing work as in social work and we can in fact see the effect in microcosm if we look at those Institute members who worked for housing associations. After the Second World War housing associations consisted of a few large trusts (e.g. Sutton, Guinness and Peabody) which had in fact always tended to be male dominated, and a much larger number of medium or small associations and trusts, many of them old established, growing only slowly and with often a very heavy emphasis on a 'caring role'. In the 1960s and 70s the injection, first of all of much larger charitable funds through Shelter, and then of central government money, produced a 'new generation' of housing associations – faster growing because dependent on growth for survival and often putting on a more 'business image' to attract funds.

These became predominantly, though not always, managed by men. It is also interesting to note that since 1974 the associations have become ever more closely linked with the Housing Corporation – a body which has never had a woman chairman and has had no women in its top ranks of management.

This view of a change in the balance of influence within the housing association movement is reinforced by an examination of the membership of the Council of the National Federation of Housing Associations (N.F.H.A.).[25] In 1946 the Council consisted of five women and 14 men. As Figure 9.2 indicates even by 1966 there were only four women council members (out of 25). The Figure shows how this rose slightly in the next couple of years and then dropped sharply, with no women left on the council in 1974. There has been a slight revival since then which makes the pattern look very similar to that of the Institute's Council (Figure 9.1). It seems reasonable to suppose that similar factors were acting on each. It is interesting to note also that, as with the central government bodies (see Chapter 10) the power to co-opt was not used in the N.F.H.A. to redress the balance. Of 63 co-options over the period only nine were used in favour of women (eight in fact were for the same person). Though membership of the Council is not an exact reflection of the participation in individual associations it is a reflection of the balance of influence within the housing association movement.

One of the additional factors, therefore, which would have worked against women in housing and particularly those in senior positions, was the growth in size in housing organisations, the increasing scope of senior positions and the higher salaries. Women can themselves share preconceptions about their role – in this case lack of confidence in their ability to manage large organisations.

"Women tended to do better in the smaller offices. I don't think on the whole that many women are very good at an enormous canvas."
"How far can women really delegate?"

We have already mentioned, in discussion of the fall of women's representation on the Institute of Housing Council, the feeling that women were less willing to compete fiercely for status. This factor was also felt to be important in affecting women who might have aimed for top jobs in housing. To some extent this reflects stereotyped views and is not entirely born out by evidence. Recent studies have suggested that it is only in specific situations that men are more competitive and dominant than women.[26] Much dispute centres around whether this is an innate or conditioned attribute. It obviously became important in the post 1960 stage when housing jobs, as we have seen, became larger, better paid and more attractive to men. Women had to be more

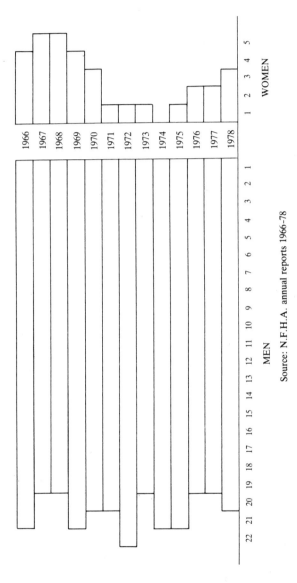

Source: N.F.H.A. annual reports 1966-78

Figure 9.2
Men and women members of N.F.H.A. council 1966–78

competitive to get to the top as these comments by women Society members indicate.

"There are so many women in my experience who just didn't (partly their own fault) . . . they wouldn't make it to the top . . . because they perhaps hadn't even enough confidence in their ability to do so."

"– a lot of them were content with job satisfaction, it never occurred to them to go higher."

"One of the differences between men and women I think, men are more career conscious, conscious of status."

"Women have much tougher endurance than men but I've found in working life that few are prepared to go on and on (competing for promotion) and not give up and get discouraged."

In addition to the evidence from Walton's study of social work the reduction in the numbers of women in top posts when organisations become larger and jobs become better paid has been well documented in education. For example the proportion of principals of Colleges of Education who were women fell from 63 per cent in 1965 to 43 per cent in 1973; deputy principals from 68 per cent to 40 per cent.[27] Eileen Byrne shows how this coincided with the move to larger, urban and coeducational institutions. She points out that this is of greater significance educationally than the simple case of personal injustice to women academics. "It means . . . the lack of an adequate feminine or feminist voice in the constant restructuring of higher education."[28] She also points out that it means a lack of role models to lift the horizons of women students.

It is also interesting to note that in one or two professions which did not suffer this kind of reorganisation into larger units the proportion of women actually rose over similar periods. The number of female barristers increased from 3.2 per cent in 1955 to 8.7 per cent in 1978 and female solicitors from 2.0 per cent in 1967 to 6.5 per cent in 1976/77. In 1976 15 per cent of dentists were women and there was felt to have been a slight increase since then.[29] The decline in the proportion of qualified women in housing was therefore not part of an overall decline in the participation of women in other professions.

Housing management policy

Another factor which could have been influential in this period is more specific to housing. We have already commented on the somewhat ambiguous position in which housing as an occupation stands regarding sex role stereotyping. Women are 'acceptable' in caring roles and it was particularly the caring and social aspect of housing which was emphasised in the 'Octavia Hill' tradition. Yet, as has already been mentioned, in the late 1950s and early 1960s there seems to have been a strong current against this kind of concept of the housing service: the view that local authorities were only there to provide the buildings and that tenants no longer needed 'wet nursing' was more vigorously propounded. The 'social role' of housing has always had a more troubled fate than that of education or the personal social services. The long fight to gain acceptance of state intervention in the property market has been well documented but political ideology plays an important part in all changes in housing. Is it a coincidence that the position of women seemed to be in decline when the 'social role' of housing was in eclipse? Is it a coincidence that the number of women qualifying is rising at a time when a number of factors have brought a re-emphasis on the social role of housing management? It would be a mistake to accept any too simplistic an argument: a number of complex factors and changes over time seem to have been at work. Nevertheless, it will be interesting to see whether, in the next decade, women improve their share of housing jobs, especially in the senior posts, and what relationship this bears to the size of housing organisations and to their social role.

Discrimination?
Some of the women interviewed said that they did not feel that they had been discriminated against as women. This statement, however, was in many cases followed by the statement that women had to work harder than men to 'prove themselves'.

"No, I've never had any prejudice against me as a woman, in fact I prefer working in a mixed sex office."

"I think I had to fight harder for promotion than the men and I certainly felt after amalgamation particularly that one had to be twice as good as a man to be recognised, but once I was accepted I found it a distinct advantage being a woman. . . ."

Others, while not wishing to generalise too much, recognised that being a woman had affected their career in this way.

"Oh I think so, for one thing it was harder to get jobs and you had to push more than you would have done naturally . . . in local government you had to convince them all the time that you could do it . . . until they got used to you."

"I think that like most women in the profession I've probably had to work a bit harder because one is up against so much prejudice about women's attitude to things – men do take a stance."

"People may make assumptions about how you will react as a woman."

"I think when it came from going up from deputy to director of housing then it would be a disadvantage – but not necessarily."

Often interviewees knew that the way had been paved for them by an earlier woman housing manager – the difficulties occurred in facing councils who had never employed a woman before or upon local government amalgamation when the two different traditions met:

"It was an accepted thing in X that there were women housing managers and there had been since (. . .) and we were given the responsibility although we weren't paid adequately. But after amalgamation the other two boroughs had been mainly men and I think they thought we were a rather peculiar kind of animal – and you know they just couldn't take it – that we knew as much about housing management and building construction as they did – they thought it was most odd and it took them some time to realise it . . . it wasn't hostility it was just sort of blank surprise in a way."

Three of the women interviewees made no statements of this type – in examining their careers it seemed in fact that they had made relatively smooth progress upwards.

Cases of discrimination against women in employment have been notoriously difficult to prove.[30] Two of the women interviewed could quote very open examples of discrimination against them prior to the Equal Opportunities legislation. On the whole, as we have seen, interviewees wanted to play down this aspect but as one of them said, "The decisions of appointing bodies must bear some responsibility."

Conclusions

The relative changes in the employment of qualified men and women in housing which are indicated by the membership and other statistics, therefore, seem to be the result of a complex series of interactions and cannot be held to be the result of the demise of the Society alone. Nevertheless, before ending this chapter it is useful to look at the evidence of the interviewees on the positive contribution which the Society made to the employment of women in housing. Besides the general propaganda for women's employment in housing, largely carried out in the pre 1948 period, the interviews provided evidence of two other important factors – general 'social support' and the provision of role models.

It is clear from many of the extracts given earlier that the general 'support' given by the Society to its members was considerable. The system of training, usually in two offices and often moving on to a third soon after training, ensured that people had a nucleus of fellow members whom they knew. The emphasis on a common tradition and view of housing management (though there was room for much variation in this) helped to make for a cohesive group, as did the relatively small size of the Society. This group support was obviously important to a large number of its members, even those who saw the 'narrow minded' or 'smug' aspects of the Society's character. It helped to sustain members when they were working in relatively isolated conditions. Most interviewees also paid tribute to the intellectual calibre of this group.

Secondly, training through the Society helped to provide younger women with 'role models' – examples of women who had achieved success in their field. Even if students found the character of a particular manager unsympathetic they subsequently, through training and career patterns, encountered others whom they could admire. When Society interviewees were asked 'Can you name a person or persons who had been influential in your career?', they all named women whom they had encountered as senior staff in the early days of their career, or 'the Society in general'. One or two mentioned others such as a headmaster who had introduced information on the Society but the evidence for the influence of Society members was overwhelming. Institute interviewees tended to be much less specific, though one or two did mention the influence of admired senior staff.

The importance of such 'role models' for underachieving groups has been particularly discussed in relation to the educational achievement of black children in a white dominated society.[31] The view that similar factors are important for women is one of the reasons why considerable attention has been given by feminists in recent years to images of women presented in the media and in education.[32] Senior members of the Society provided 'adult role models' demonstrating that women could succeed in housing.[33] It should also be noted, however, that as in other occupational areas, some men in senior positions did encourage women staff to seek qualification and more senior positions.

What then of the future? There has certainly been some improvement in the position of women in the Council and in the numbers of women students qualifying. However, if the factors mentioned above are taken seriously the future must seem cloudy, if not black. The Institute, by its nature, cannot provide propaganda for the employment of women. Does it provide any of the support which women obtained from the Society, or is this no longer necessary? In most branch meetings and in all Chief Officers' and Institute meetings women are in a minority – often a very small one. So it does not seem likely that the same degree of support is present. Nor is it providing the role models which play such an important part in encouraging younger women. Many of the 'older generation' are near, or have reached, retirement age. The picture we can piece together indicates that the next generation of Directors and Assistant Directors will contain far fewer women than the previous one. If this is the case students will lack that kind of encouragement from seeing women in senior positions which so many studies have shown is vitally needed. On the other hand, to take a more optimistic view, it is clear that the majority of women are now being trained in mixed offices. They will not now suffer from the differences in 'culture' between the Society and the Institute. Will this generation therefore be better able to compete with men? More information about the current position would help.

Finally, it must be remembered that in the last three chapters we have been looking at the role and employment of those women who were lucky enough to achieve a professional qualification. They are a relatively privileged and small group compared with most of the women employed in housing. As Chapter 5 showed women have been almost exclusively employed in the lower grades of housing organisations doing routine, though often demanding, jobs. Even those with educational qualifications are not employed on equivalent grades as men with the same type of qualification. The relatively disadvantaged position of the qualified women only mirrors the more disadvantaged position of the majority of employed women whose hopes of reaching more interesting and better paid jobs in housing are at present extremely slim.

References
1. For example M. Sherif and C. Sherif. *Groups in Harmony and Tension,* Harper, New York, 1953.
2. M. Argyle. *The Psychology of Interpersonal Behaviour,* Penguin, 1967, p. 71.

3. J. Freeman (ed.). 'The Women's Liberation Movement: Its Origins, Organisation, Activities and Ideas', in *Women, A Feminist Perspective,* Mayfield, California, 1979, p. 563.
4. M. P. Ryan. 'The Power of Women's Networks', *Feminist Studies,* Vol. 5, No. 1, Spring 1979, p. 69.
5. See, for example, M. Fogarty, A. Allen, J. Allen, P. Walters. *Women in Top Jobs,* P.E.P. and George Allen and Unwin 1971, in particular 'Women in two large companies' and 'The Woman Director'.
6. See C.S.O. *Social Trends,* No. 4, H.M.S.O., 1973, p. 9.
7. See, for example M. W. Zapoleaon. 'Women in the Professions' *Journal of Social Issues,* 1950, Vol. 6, Part 3, pp. 20–24 and M. Fogarty *et. al. Women in Top Jobs, op. cit.*
8. M. Fogarty *et al. op. cit.,* pp. 278–79.
9. See J. S. Hyde and B. G. Rosenberg. *Half the Human Experience,* D. C. Heath and Co., 1976, Ch. 5, for a discussion of the relevant factors.
10. M. E. Tabor. *Octavia Hill (Pioneer Women),* The Sheldon Press, London, 1927, pp. 12–13.
11. *Ibid.*
12. Beatrice Webb. *My Apprenticeship,* Penguin, 1971, p. 281.
13. Society of Women Housing Estate Managers. Evidence to C.H.A.C. sub-committee, Public Record Office HLG 37 4.
14. E. France. 'Will new municipal Housing Estates become slums?' *Municipal Journal and Public Works Engineer,* October 18, 1935, p. 1881.
15. M. Miller, Secretary of S.W.H.E.M. Letter to *Municipal Journal and Public Works Engineer,* November 1935, p. 1985.
16. I. E. Hort, Housing Manager, Cheltenham. Letter to *Municipal Journal and Public Works Engineer,* November 1, 1935.
17. L. W. Mascall, Housing Welfare Officer, Dudley. Letter, *Ibid.* November 22, 1935.
18. J. Thompson. Letter to *Municipal Journal and Public Works Engineer,* November 1935, p. 2211.
19. *Ibid.*
20. See 'Women Architects Demand a Better Deal', *The Architects Journal,* 21 June 1978.
21. E.O.C. *Research Bulletin,* Winter 1978/9, p. 68.
22. For discussion of management seen as a male preserve see, E. N. Glenn and R. L. Feldberg. 'Clerical Work: The Female Occupation', in *Women, a Feminist Perspective, op. cit.,* pp. 313–35.
23. R. G. Walton. *Women in Social Work,* Routledge and Kegan Paul 1975, p. 261.
24. *Ibid.,* p. 238.
25. National Federation of Housing Associations. *Annual Reports,* 1965–78.
26. E. E. Maccoby and C. N. Jacklin. *The Psychology of Sex Differences,* London, Oxford University Press, 1975, pp. 247–254.
27. E. M. Bryne. *Women and Education,* Tavistock Publications, 1978, p. 224.
28. *Ibid.,* p. 225.
29. E.O.C. *Research Bulletin,* Winter 1978/9, p. 68.
30. J. Coussins. *The Equality Report,* National Council for Civil Liberties, London 1976, p. 52. "The relatively low number of *Sex Discrimination Act* cases does not mean that most employers have stopped discriminating on grounds of sex. The problem is partly one of proving the discrimination. . . ."
31. B. Coard. *How the West Indian Child is made educationally subnormal in the British school system,* New Beacon Books Ltd, London 1971, pp. 28–31.
32. For example through the formation of the Women in the Media Group and the work of the Women in Education Group.
33. L. Davidson and L. Kramer Gordon. *The Sociology of Gender,* Rand McNalley College Publishing Co. U.S.A. 1979, pp. 24–25 discusses the importance of adult role models in education.

CHAPTER 10

Councillors, Members of Parliament and Pressure Groups

The preceding chapters have been concerned with the participation of women as staff of housing organisations. But at both central and local levels of government numerous other groups are involved in policy making – councillors, Members of Parliament, Ministers of the Crown, members of advisory committees and pressure groups. The balance of power between the groups at national and local level will vary from time to time but most commentators agree that it is these groups, along with their employed staffs, which determine the policies of central and local government. Therefore the relative powerlessness of women in housing employment could be counterbalanced by the presence of women in powerful positions in these other bodies. How far is this so? In this chapter the available evidence about the contribution of women in these other policy making bodies is examined looking first at local government, then at central government and finally at pressure groups. The particular position with regard to housing is then compared with other areas of public policy. But we did not research the membership of committees of management of housing associations. The outcome of this study suggests that the presence of women in these other influential bodies does not compensate for their lack of influence within the housing organisations. Many of those factors which affect their participation in housing organisations apply equally to their involvement in these other bodies.

Local government

Participation of women as elected representatives

Before enquiring how far women occupy positions of influence in local government it is worth considering briefly their general participation as elected representatives.

Despite the fairly widespread belief that councillors are mostly elderly men and middle aged housewives, there are remarkably few women in local government. The most recent large survey, carried out in 1976 for the Robinson committee on the remuneration of councillors, showed that out of a representative sample of about 5000 councillors, only 17 per cent were women.[1] The committee commented on this under-representation in view of the fact that women make up more than 50 per cent of the population. An earlier survey done for the Maud committee had shown that in 1964 12 per cent of councillors were women.[2] So a decade had not brought any great change in the composition of local councils. Councillors in 1976 still tended to be "predominantly male, middle aged and middle class".[3] However, the slight increase in the number of female councillors since 1964 has been among those under 55.[4] This is interesting because at the time of the Maud committee women councillors tended to be older than men councillors.

A recent study by Stephen Bristow in 1977 shows that the highest percentage of women councillors occurs in Conservative County Councils.[5] He maintains that the best single indicator of the likelihood of a high level of female representation is the strength of the Conservative party in County government. He also noted that women were better represented in affluent residential areas, especially in the South of England, than elsewhere. But a study of London Boroughs between 1968 and 1973 produced evidence that in London the Conservative party had "a lower representation of women than either the Labour party or the more fluid minority parties".[6] There may therefore be specific reasons why there are more women councillors in some areas than others. In the absence of more evidence it is not possible to explain why this should be so.

Thus it seems that over the last 15 years, despite greater 'feminist' activity, there has been little improvement in the representation of women in local government. Even where there are women representatives they are more likely than not to be middle aged and middle class. Bristow concludes that it is because of women's traditionally subordinate status that they fail to develop those skills and motivations which would encourage them to play a more dominant role in politics.

One reason advanced by the Maud committee for the paucity of women councillors was the fact that women were shown to be much less likely to be members of an organisation. Half of all councillors had been brought into touch with council work initially through their membership of an organisation. This may well also be linked with our findings in the previous chapter about the different 'style' of organisation that women adopt. Our own experience in one East London Borough was that the women there definitely adopted a more informal, flexible and less official form of organisation. Such organisations found difficulty in obtaining recognition from 'the establishment'. Working class women in particular seem to find formal organisation of meetings with officers and constitutions off-putting. This may well be the reason why a growth in community activity, often involving women, is not paralleled by a rise in the number of women councillors.

Similar difficulties have been experienced by women's organisations seeking to obtain official funding, for example to maintain refuges for battered wives. In order to satisfy the 'rules' they may have to organise themselves in a way which does not reflect their own values. This matter will be touched on again in the section on pressure groups.

Who are the leaders in local government?
The fact that in 1976 only 17 per cent of councillors were women meant that the pool from which candidates could be drawn for offices carrying influence and power was small. But did an equivalent proportion achieve these offices? The Robinson committee studied four positions which seemed to bear recognised leadership. These were chairman, mayor (or equivalent) of the council; vice-chairman or deputy mayor; majority party leader; chairman or convener of a committee. They found that women were less well represented than men in these offices since only 12 per cent were women.[7]

The study of four London Boroughs undertaken by the Greater London Group at the London School of Economics found a similarly small proportion of women to be leaders.[8] Defining a leader as a chairman or vice-chairman of a committee, one in six were women. Interestingly, however, they record that in one particular Borough (Newham) there were several women in the dominant leadership groups in the 1950s. They suggest that "Their pre-eminence may have been associated with the leading role that women played in that area as street wardens in the Second World War and in the period of reconstruction that followed, and even with the strong tradition of feminism in the East End during the suffragette movement."[9] It would be interesting to know if this were the case elsewhere.

Considering the position of women generally as leaders it seems that their influence is not great. Their position more specifically in relation to housing as compared with other services can be seen most clearly if we examine the position of women as chairmen of committees.[10]

Women as chairmen of major committees
The first fact to be noted was that in 1977 41 per cent of councils had no woman chairman of any major committee. ('Major committee' was defined as social services, housing, public or environmental health, recreation facilities and amenities, planning/development and policy.) This was at its most marked among District Councils where in 159 (43 per cent) authorities no major committee was chaired by a woman.

Only 12 per cent of all major committees in local authorities had a woman as chairman in 1977. This was slightly higher than in the previous year (11 per cent). Figure 10.1 shows how these women chairmen were distributed between the different service areas. Social services with its traditional 'helping' image was clearly considered the most suitable area for women and 29 per cent of committees were chaired by a woman. The only other service which came close to having the same number of women chairmen was education. Housing was in an intermediate position since slightly less than one fifth (19 per cent) of housing chairmanships were held by a woman in both 1976 and 1977. As Table 10.1 shows women were more likely to be found as chairman of a housing committee in a District Council than in a London Borough.

The Maud committee commented that the importance attached to housing in the hierarchy of committees varied between authorities. They suggested that where housing provision was already adequate it may well be that housing

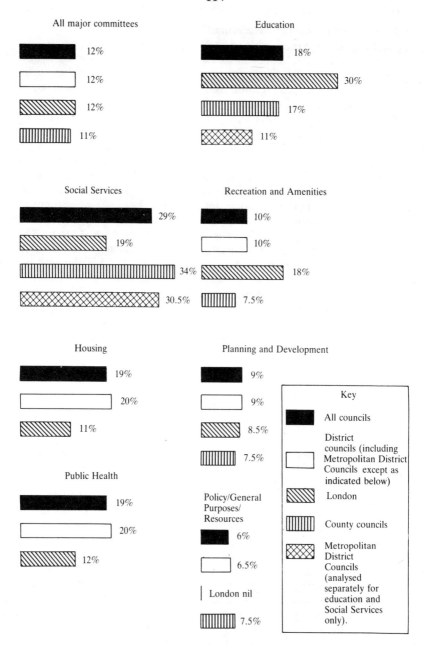

Figure 10.1
Percentage of major committees chaired by a woman in 1977: England and Wales

Table 10.1

Percentage of housing committees chaired by a woman in 1977: England and Wales

	No. of housing committees*	No. of housing committees with a woman as chairman	% of housing committees with a woman as chairman
District Councils	378	74	20
London	36	4	11
Total	414	78	19

* Some authorities had 2 committees for housing.

does not seem to be of great significance. Reasons why housing was considered very important in some local authorities included the amount of capital expenditure on building, public interest in the subject, rent policies and the waiting list. Could this be the reason why women are more likely to be chairmen of housing committees in District Councils than in the higher spending London authorities where housing often arouses considerable political passion? Since the Maud committee reported other issues such as homelessness, problems over difficult-to-let accommodation and the sale of council housing have combined to make the chairman's position even more of a 'hot seat'. While no direct evidence is available, the general argument that the chairman is less likely to be a woman if the committee is a powerful one is borne out by the practice of the most powerful committees in local government, the policy and resources committees.

The growth of policy and resources committees follows from a recommendation of the Bains committee.[11] The latter's intention was that a new committee should co-ordinate policy and be responsible for strategic financial matters. A study by INLOGOV comparing local authority committees in 1967 with those in 1974–75 shows the great growth of these new combined committees.[12] Here again the number of women chairmen was very small. In 1977 only six per cent of councils had a woman as chairman of this committee while in London (again) the picture was even blacker, with not one woman holding this position. This is indeed a very significant finding. With the growth of the idea of corporate management the power of the centralising committees has become proportionately greater and that of the 'service committees' less. Particularly in times of financial stringency the overall standards will be set by the policy and resources committee, leaving the service committee less room for manoeuvre. The fact that in London no woman was chairman of such a committee is a graphic illustration of the argument that the greater the amount of power exercised the fewer the number of women involved.

Why are women not more influential in local government?
We have examined the position of women as chairmen of housing and other major committees and seen that social services with its 'caring' image was the

only committee to have a higher proportion of women chairmen than housing. The more powerful the committee the less likely there was to be a woman chairman. This corresponds to our findings in the previous chapters – that women are acceptable in a 'caring' role but as organisations grow bigger and power becomes greater they are less likely to be chosen for positions of responsibility.

Factors affecting the choice of chairmen of local government committees were studied by the Maud committee. While political party was the most important influence on who became chairman, another factor, seniority, might have the effect of excluding women who have interrupted their political careers by having children. Women may also be affected by the amount of time involved in being a chairman – estimated at 98 hours per month by the Robinson committee. Once on a committee it seems that women on average spend slightly more time than men on council activities (81 hours per month compared with 78 for men).

There seems no evidence that authorities attempt to achieve a balance. There used to be a statutory duty for welfare committees to include a woman but this is no longer the case since the establishment of social service committees.[13] As far back as 1944, the Central Housing Advisory Committee deplored the absence of women on housing committees. "We find that she [the housewife] is still inadequately represented on many local authorities and we should like to see much fuller use by local authorities of their powers to co-opt suitable women to their housing committees."[14] The political sensitivity of the housing service is probably one of the many factors which militates against this. In any case, co-opted members are unlikely to reach positions of real power. The Maud committee commented "And in an activity so much concerned with the amelioration of family and social problems can the proportion of women councillors (only 12 per cent) be considered satisfactory?"[15]

It is clear that apart from any special reasons which may affect the choice of a particular person as chairman, the main reason for the low level of women's influence in local government is their overall lack of numbers. Most of the studies concerning women's participation in local government were carried out some time ago in a very different social climate. Yet the growth in the number of employed women and the growth in feminism have not been paralleled by a growth in participation in local government. Indeed the first factor may militate against it, for a woman who is coping with a full-time job as well as a home has even less time to devote to political activity. These practical considerations may be accentuated by the preference for more informal organisations and the feeling of having to penetrate into a 'male club' – a feeling which as we will see is even more marked at central government level.

Central government

Ministers and Members of Parliament

The scarcity of women M.P.s is well documented and the reasons for this have been comprehensively explored in a recent work.[16] Only four per cent of M.P.s (in 1977) were women, so the position was even worse in Parliament than in the local authorities even though a woman became Prime Minister in 1979. In Parliament, too, as Table 10.2 shows, fewer women reached positions of influence in Housing than in some other services, notably Health and Social Services departments or in Education. No woman has been Minister of Housing and few women, from either the House of Commons or the House of Lords, have served even in a junior capacity in the Ministry. In fact Housing compares badly with other Ministries. Only five women have held a post in the Ministry since women became eligible in 1924 to sit as M.P.s.

Table 10.2

Ministerial posts held by women* 1924–1977

Education	13
Health/Pensions/National Insurance/Health and Social Security/Social Services	12
Foreign Office/Commonwealth/Colonial/Overseas Development	9
Labour/Employment/Trade/Transport/Prices	7
Home Office	5
Environment (including Housing and Public Building and Works and two who served in the Ministry of Health which was responsible for housing 1919–1951)	5
Scottish/Welsh Office	5
Food/Agriculture, Fish and Food	3
Others (including Whips and Baronesses-in-Waiting)	16
Total	75

* A total of 35 women held these 75 posts. They came from both the House of Commons and the House of Lords.

Women, of course, have only been eligible to sit in the House of Commons since 1918. In 1958 women were also admitted to the House of Lords as Life Peers, and in 1963 hereditary Peeresses were allowed to enter the Lords. They have already proved their value in relation to housing matters, since one member (Lady Summerskill) was responsible for two important Private Members Bills which originated in the Upper House. These were the *Married Women's Property Act 1964* and the *Matrimonial Homes Act 1967*.

The potential importance of women in the Houses of Parliament does not need stressing. The reasons for their absence have been extensively described elsewhere and include the feeling of intrusion into a 'male club', which we mentioned in the previous chapter. Although women M.P.s have often tried to fight the idea of being confined to 'women's issues' as we have seen in Table 10.2, housing is once again seen as more of a male preserve.

Enid Lakeman, Director of the Electoral Reform Society, suggests that one reason for the smaller number of women in national, compared with local, politics is "because a woman's family responsibilities are more easily combined with local political work than with serving in the possibly far distant capital".[17] She believes that proportional representation might increase the number of women. She considers that in single member constituencies there is a feeling that a woman might lose men's votes but that with multi-member there would be "pressure in the opposite direction – not to offend either sex by excluding it but to widen the party's appeal by including both".[18] That is 'balancing the ticket'.

Members of advisory committees

Housing policy, however, at central level has not remained the sole prerogative of elected members and civil servants. Other people have been involved as well, often through formal or informal committees. Most Ministries have a network of such committees attached to them. They can take a number of forms. Usually they are ad hoc (appointed for a particular purpose) or standing (permanent, though the members may change). There has been considerable controversy about the influence these committees exert. In one of the earliest research studies Kenneth Wheare described their functions as to advise, to inquire, to negotiate, to legislate, to administer, to scrutinise and to control.[19]

A later study by P.E.P. focused solely on committees to advise.[20] Included among what they called "Fifteen major committees" was one concerned with housing. This was the Central Housing Advisory Committee whose powers included that of taking the initiative in topics. The P.E.P. report said "It is also sometimes argued that the power of initiative is the key to an advisory committee's strength."[21] However this would not necessarily ensure a good hearing for a committee's views for, as P.E.P. said, "departments are not likely to be enthusiastic about advice on subjects they do not want to hear about".[22]

To what extent were women involved in this committee? Few have analysed committees according to the sex of the membership. What follows is an analysis of the Central Housing Advisory Committee and its sub-committees – in terms of the contribution made by women. This analysis is based on a study of all the reports produced by this body.

The Central Housing Advisory Committee: 1935–75. This committee was in existence for exactly 40 years. Set up in 1935 to advise the Minister responsible for housing on matters of practice and policy, it was disbanded in 1975. Although it had detailed terms of reference it could also make general representations to the Minister.[23] The influence of this committee, particularly on matters of design (for example setting housing standards in the recommendations of the Dudley and Parker Morris sub-committees) has been considerable.[24] Although it has usually restricted its attention to non-political aspects of housing there have been exceptions: "In 1953 it produced a report supporting differential rents – by no means a non-political topic."[25]

The topics covered by the committee (summarised in Figure 10.2) range from design, unsatisfactory tenants, management and housing associations to rural housing, the needs of new communities and the selection of tenants. The committee worked through sub-committees (28 in all) and members were appointed to be, in Mary Smith's words, "experts in different aspects of housing".[26] When the membership of these sub-committees, however, is examined closely, an interesting picture emerges. An analysis of chairman, members and officers of these 28 sub-committees shows clearly what role women have played. Only 27 of the 28 sub-committees had a chairman, the other one consisting of four members of equal status. Of these 27 sub-committees 25 had a man as chairman. The exceptions were sub-committees chaired by the Dowager Marchioness of Reading in 1959 and Mrs (later Dame) E. Denington in 1966. The members were appointed by the Minister, usually after consultation with the appropriate representative organisations. Some sub-committees, however, had power to co-opt. Over the 40 years of their existence these sub-committees had 289 members, of whom 70 (24 per cent) were women. But as Figure 10.2 shows, they were not equally spread between the sub-committees. Two sub-committees had *no* women on them. These were:

1939   *The demolition of individual unfit houses in rural areas* (Chairman: The Bishop of Winchester)

1971   *Housing Associations* (Chairman: Sir K. Cohen)

The absence of a woman from the latter is particularly surprising given the early and continued involvement of women in housing associations.

At the other extreme two sub-committees had women as half their members:

1947   *Rural Housing* (Chairman: Sir A. Hobhouse)

1965   *The First Hundred Families* (the sub-committee which had no chairman)

In no case did the number of women ever exceed one half.

There is no pattern to the balance between the sexes. For example, the number of women might have been expected to increase as women became more involved in public affairs. However, Figure 10.2 indicates that there is no steady or consistent growth in the numbers of women. The proportion of women zigzags up and down, plummeting with the last sub-committee which contained no women.

A closer examination of the 70 women members shows that a number served on more than one committee. In fact only 30 women were involved. Miss (later Lady) Megan Lloyd George, M.P., for example, served on seven sub-committees and both the Dowager Marchioness of Reading and Mrs E. Gooch served on six. Eight other women served on between three and five sub-committees. Of the 219 male members 95 names recur, which is almost exactly the same proportion of men as of women serving on several sub-committees.[27] So for both men and women a quite small overall number is involved.

In 22 of the sub-committee reports the names of staff were also given. Here women did better, being nearly half (45 per cent). But again there were wide variations. Nine (41 per cent) sub-committees had no woman as secretary or

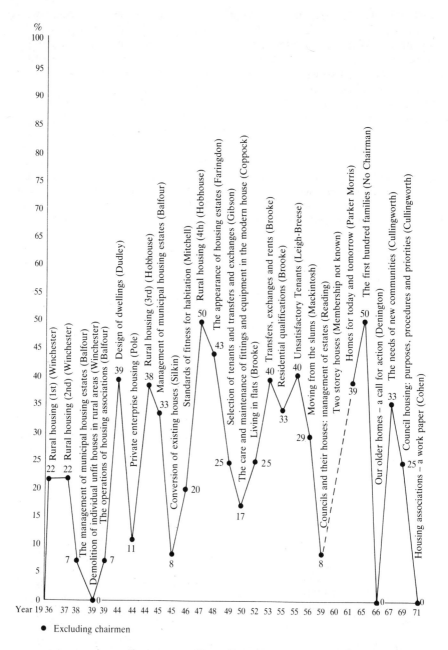

● Excluding chairmen

Figure 10.2
Central Housing Advisory Committees 1935–75 percentage of members* who were women
(with names of committees and chairmen in brackets)

assistant secretary while in four cases (18 per cent) all the named staff were women.

A more recent example of a standing advisory group is the Housing Services Advisory Group. Set up in 1976 the membership has remained basically the same with one or two variations. The group has fluctuated between 14 and 17 members but the two women members have remained the same. The percentage of women has therefore remained stable at about 12 to 14 per cent. The chairman has been a civil servant (a man) who was a Deputy Secretary in the Department of the Environment.

Ad hoc national committees. Governments often set up ad hoc committees to look at particular problems. Taking the ten year period 1965–75 the five ad hoc committees concerned with housing were:

1965 *The Committee on Housing in Greater London* (Chairman: Sir Milner Holland) (Cmnd. 2605).

1971 *The Committee on the Rent Acts* (Chairman: Mr H. Francis) Cmnd. 4609).

1974 *The Advisory Committee on Rent Rebates and Rent Allowances* (Chairman: Professor B. Cullingworth)

1975 *The Working Party on Housing Co-operatives* (Chairman: Mr H. Campbell)

1977 *The Advisory Committee on Rent Rebates and Allowances* (Chairman: Professor B. Cullingworth)

None of the chairmen were women and, as Table 10.3 shows, few women (from none to one quarter) were members:

Table 10.3

Ad hoc national housing committees 1965–77 – women members

Committee	Members*	Women	% who were women
Milner Holland	11	2	18
Francis	4	1	25
Cullingworth	11	1	9
Campbell	7	0	0
Cullingworth	17	4	24

* Excluding chairman.

As far as staff were concerned the position was even more dismal. The names of secretaries were given in the case of Milner Holland, Francis and Campbell. All were men.

In addition to these five committees there was an ad hoc Advisory Group set up to advise the Minister over the Housing Policy Review. This resulted in the *Housing Policy* Consultative Document 1977. The chairman was the Minister and there were 15 non-government members, including two women. There were two sub-groups, one with two women members (out of ten) and the other none (out of eight).

Table 10.4

Housing policy review committees – women members

Committee	Total members	Women	% who were women
Housing Policy Review Advisory Group	15	2	13
Working Group on new forms of social ownership	10	2	20
Working Group on house purchase finance	8	0	0

Taking all the eight committees which have just been mentioned together there were a total of 83 members of whom 12 were women (14 per cent). But two of these served twice and so there were only ten women involved. As has been seen none of these eight committees had a woman chairman.

Committees connected with the New Towns. New Towns are run by committees appointed by the Minister. Seventeen had their own separate committee in 1977 and four were grouped under a single Commission.

Of the 17 committees most had between six and seven members. As far as women committee members are concerned, Harlow had none, 12 of the others had one woman member and four had two women members. In most cases, therefore, the 'token woman' appeared, but the overall figure of 17 per cent for women members of New Town committees indicates a situation in which women have very little influence indeed. The remaining four New Towns (Crawley, Hatfield, Hemel Hempstead and Welwyn Garden City) were grouped under the Commission for New Towns. In 1977 all the six members, chairman and deputy chairman were men and so was the secretary.

The membership of the advisory committees concerned with housing and the New Town committees have been examined in detail because they illustrate an important point. Membership is by appointment and is always part time, so many of the usual arguments against the participation of women, especially married women, do not apply. There is no need to stand for election and the hours are not necessarily onerous. As has been seen, however, this has made no difference. A proportionate number of women was not appointed, nor does there seem to be any rhyme or reason for the actual numbers of women appointed to the various committees.

Pressure groups

The Guardian Directory of Pressure Groups and Representative Associations defines a pressure group as "an association of individuals joined together by a common interest, belief, activity or purpose that seeks to achieve its objectives, further its interests and enhance its status in relation to other groups, by gaining the approval and co-operation of authority in the form of favourable policies, legislation and conditions".[28] It would be beyond the scope of this study to look in detail at all the relevant pressure groups listed in the Directory but the three major ones concerned with housing are: the Campaign for the Homeless and Rootless (C.H.A.R.), the Simon Community Trust and Shelter. The Directory gives their aims and the names of some of their staff. In addition we note the membership of an independent housing organisation (The Housing Centre Trust) which also, on occasions, acts as a pressure group.

C.H.A.R. states its aims as "To enforce and extend existing rights to housing, social services and employment for Britain's single homeless people and bring together in united action those voluntary bodies who at present care for the homeless and rootless." They listed their chairman and director. Both were men.

The Simon Community Trust says that its aims are "To assist and care for homeless and rootless people who have additional social problems – mental illness, recidivists, sexual deviants, drug dependency etc." They listed the founder, chairman, secretary/treasurer and press/public relations officer. All were men.

Shelter is probably one of the best known groups in any field. They see their role as "To provide assistance for people in Britain without proper homes or without homes at all by promoting housing associations, housing aid centres, city improvement projects, influencing policy and public education." Patrick Rivers describing their role after eight years said "The organisation is a long way from enjoying the cherished status of automatic consultation" but that nevertheless some staff had developed close contacts with civil servants and were able to give advice and information.[29] Again there has been little involvement at the top by women. Listed in the *Guardian Directory* are the Board of Management (four men), the director (a man) and eight officers, of whom six were men. The two women were the information officer and the research director.

The Housing Centre Trust is a non-political, non-sectarian body committed to the improvement of housing conditions. In 1977 one quarter (5 out of 20) of its council were women and so were both principal officers.

There has been a growth also of local pressure groups but there is no information available about how many women are involved. One notes that the major national pressure groups concerned with housing, like the other housing organisations, are nearly all run by men. Women may be working extensively in the field but when it comes to the influential positions they do not appear. Strangely enough, the only inheritor of the position of the Society of Women Housing Managers as a body which does have a reasonable representation of women is one with very different values but once again a body which excludes men from their national decision making bodies – the National conference and the National Co-ordinating Group of the National Women's Aid Federation.This is the one body in the modern housing field which is run by women, and it has received some official recognition through being given grants and beginning to be included in the consultation processes. Its position is still weak, however, and there are fears within the movement which generated it that, as it begins to get a recognised status, it is moving away from its original aims and values. It is interesting that some all female organisations such as the Women's Institutes and Townswomen's Guilds have played some role in influencing committees concerned with the design of housing. (See Chapter 2.)

Pressure groups thus provide particularly interesting examples in this study of women's influence in housing and it is regrettable that more information is not available. From observation it would seem that at a local level and the lower level of organisation women participate equally with men. They are just as concerned about the plight of the homeless and ill-housed. It might have been assumed that pressure groups, being voluntary and 'progressive' bodies, would encourage an equal representation of women. Yet once again at national level and at the source of power the representation is overwhelmingly male.

Conclusions

It is amply evident in this chapter that the lack of women in employment with housing organisations is not compensated for by the presence of women in representative central and local government organisations, appointed committees or in pressure groups. While the lack of women as elected representatives is easier to understand, given the present circumstances, it is more depressing to find the pattern repeated in pressure groups concerned with a subject so important to women and to find that no attempt in an era of so-called equal opportunity, is made to redress the balance in appointed committees.

It can be argued that both the committee system and 'official' pressure groups are attempts to disarm the opposition by co-opting them – criticism can be more forceful from the outside. Unfortunately, there is little evidence that the outsider's voice is ever listened to – rather the evidence is all to the contrary.

Will women always be content to be represented by men and have these important decisions which affect their whole life decided by men? Prescriptions have been put forward for aiding the position of women in politics but some of the powerful forces which 'keep women in their place' will be discussed in the next chapter and also some of the differing ideas about what that place should be.

References
1. D.O.E. *Report of Inquiry into the system of remuneration of members of local authorities* (the Robinson report).
   Vol. 1. Report, Cmnd. 7010, H.M.S.O., 1977.
   Vol. II. The surveys of councillors and local authorities, H.M.S.O., 1977.
   Vol. II gives the results of a survey of all local authorities in Great Britain and a survey of a representative sample of 5,061 councillors. See especially p. 5.
2. M.H.L.G. *Management of Local Government* (the Maud report), H.M.S.O., 1967:
   Vol. 1. *Report of the Committee.*
   Vol. 2. *The Local Government Councillor.*
   Vol. 3. *The Local Government Elector.*

Vol. 4. *Local Government Administration Abroad.*
Vol. 5. *Local Government Administration in England and Wales.*
See in particular Chap. 7 of vol. 5.The committee carried out a survey of 4,043 councillors. See especially Vol. 5, pp. 19–20.
3. Robinson report. *op cit.,* Vol. 1, p. 11.
4. Robinson report. *op. cit.,* Vol. 11, p. 5.
5. S. Bristow. 'Women Councillors', *County Councils Gazette,* May, November and December 1978.
6. Greater London Group, London School of Economics. As part of a research study comparing local political structures and processes in four London Boroughs a survey of councillors was undertaken. This was based on a questionnaire sent to 418 councillors. The findings about women are on p. 3 of chap. 5, of their unpublished report. Some of the findings were written up by their research officer: P. Chamberlayne. 'The Coming of a new type of Member', *Municipal Review,* May 1975, pp. 6–7.
7. Robinson report. *op. cit.* Vol. II, Table 16, p. 13.
8. Greater London Group. *op. cit.*
9. *Ibid,* chap. 5, p. 4.
10. Numbers have been obtained from the Municipal Year Books which are published by the Municipal Journal Ltd. See Appendix: Sources of the Data.
11. D.O.E. *The New Local Authorities. Management and Structure* (the Bains report), H.M.S.O., 1972, Chap. 4.
12. R. Greenwood, M. A. Lomer, C. R. Hinings and S. Ranson. *The Organisation of local authorities in England and Wales, 1967–75,* University of Birmingham, Institute of Local Government Studies, 1975, p. 35.
13. Under the *National Assistance Act 1948* S.33(2) and Third Schedule Pt. 1 Welfare Committees had to include persons of special experience in welfare matters, including women, but the majority of the committee had to be members of the local authority.
14. M.O.H. C.H.A.C. *The Design of Dwellings* (the Dudley report), H.M.S.O., 1944, para. 14.
15. Maud Committee report. *op. cit.* Vol. 2, p. 289.
16. E. Vallance. *Women in the House,* The Athlone Press, 1979.
17. E. Lakeman. 'Electoral Systems and Women in Parliament', *The Parliamentarian,* Vol. 57, No. 3, p. 161.
18. *Ibid.*
19. K. C. Wheare. *Government by Committee,* Oxford University Press, 1955.
20. P.E.P. *Advisory Committees in British Government,* Allen and Unwin, 1960.
21. *Ibid.* p. 97.
22. *Ibid.*
23. *Ibid.* p. 63 and p. 160.
24. M.O.H. The Dudley report, *op. cit.,* and M.H.L.G. *Homes for Today and Tomorrow* (the Parker Morris report), H.M.S.O., 1944.
25. P.E.P. *op. cit.,* p. 81.
26. Mary E. H. Smith. *Guide to Housing,* Housing Centre Trust, 1977.
27. Five served on 7 sub-committees, 1 on 6 and 25 on between 3 and 5.
28. P. Shipley. *The Guardian Directory of Pressure Groups and Representative Associations,* Wilton House Publications, 1976, p. 3.
29. P. Rivers. *Politics by Pressure,* Harrap, 1974.

CHAPTER 11

Conclusions

Summary of findings

The previous chapters have shown that over recent years women's rights and opportunities in housing have improved significantly. From a situation where married women were automatically assumed to be dependent on their husbands and unable to hold property in their own right, women have now gained the right to hold property, they have a better chance of being able to obtain mortgages and they have more opportunities of access to public housing. They also have improved rights in regard to housing when the family home is threatened by marital breakdown. However, women still figure largely among some disadvantaged groups. In particular some elderly people and some single women who are caring for elderly relatives occupy poor housing. Other women, such as some who are battered, mentally disordered, physically disabled or homeless, suffer from unsuitable housing, lack of security or particular difficulty in becoming or remaining owner occupiers. Procedures and policies of public housing organisations are often still geared to the standard nuclear family and predetermined styles of living. Improvements can and should still be made, but substantial gains have been achieved.

On the other hand women working in the housing service are still in a very 'depressed' position. In contrast to the early days of housing work – especially at the end of the last century and beginning of this – qualified women in housing management in the 1970s have failed increasingly to secure influential positions. At the top there were only 15 women Chief Housing Officers in 1977. This represented 4 per cent compared with 9 per cent of Directors of Social Services who were women and smaller proportions in every other major service. In the "Housing Staff" study, at Principal Office level and above, only 9 per cent of staff in housing departments were women but 78 per cent of the clerical staff were women.

The proportion of qualified members of the Institute who are women has actually declined. In 1965 26 per cent were women but in 1977 this had declined to 17 per cent. There were fewer qualified women members of the Institute of Housing in 1977 (262) than there had been in 1965 (310). The only bright spot appears to be the increasing number of women students (15 per cent of students in 1965 and 24 per cent in 1977). Women now represent about one third of students qualifying, as they did in 1965 before the dip to the low point of 13 per cent in 1971.

One of the most startling changes seems to have been in housing associations. In 1965 83 per cent of all Institute members employed in associations were women but in 1977 this had dropped to 31 per cent. Looking specifically at members in senior posts in housing associations whereas in 1965 70 per cent were women in 1977 this had dropped to 27 per cent.

Nor was the picture found to be very encouraging among elected representatives at a local level. Previous surveys had found that only 17 per cent of councillors were women. We found that 41 per cent of councils had no woman chairman of any committee. Only 12 per cent of all major committees had a woman as chairman, with housing coming joint second in the list. Nineteen per cent of housing committees had a woman as chairman which was less than social services (29 per cent) and education (18 per cent) and the same as public health. All the other committees had many less.

Similarly, national government committees, the ministries and the pressure groups are all dominated by men. The key question, therefore, is why the provision of a service as important to women as this is should be tightly controlled by men and, in particular, why the improvement in access to housing has not been matched by increased influence in the way in which it is provided.

To answer this question it is necessary, first, to consider some of the underlying reasons why both access and influence have differed for men and for women. How far do these reasons arise from differences which are innate and how far are they the effect of culture? Then it is important to identify those major factors which have encouraged or retarded progress. Finally, one can go on to consider what steps should be taken to improve the position of women in housing.

The underlying causes

We can identify certain underlying factors which seem to have influenced women's access to or influence in housing. Among these are that women live longer than men, they are smaller and less muscular and that women and not men bear children. We will examine the effect of each of these and finally the effect of stereotyped sex roles.

Women live longer than men

In 20th century Britain women live, on average, longer than men. This would not necessarily be the case if there were no birth control, or if pre and post natal care was poor. This is a good example, therefore, of a factor where some aspects of human biology have been decisively affected by conditions in society. It is sometimes argued that as women increasingly take up lifelong full-time employment their mortality rates from stress related causes such as heart disease may well become similar to that of men and the balance may be readjusted.

In the meantime as far as housing is concerned women's greater longevity means that they figure more prominently in the disadvantaged groups. The physical disablement and mental confusion which some suffer as a result of ageing can cause acute housing problems. It is curious that women's longer life span brings them no corresponding advantage in relation to employment. In fact, age barriers for training and the career structures of the present time can add to the difficulties of women who return to work after caring for children or elderly relatives.

The retirement age of 60 for women is another, additional disadvantage for women, in that men in important positions have a further five years in which to exercise influence (and, incidentally, probably increase their pension) before they retire. Men, however, stress that women enjoy an additional five years of leisure. Dissatisfaction on both sides is leading to pressure for a common statutory retirement age for men and women. Whether this will improve or worsen the employment position of women remains uncertain.

The average woman is smaller and less muscular than the average man

This is a relatively well documented predominantly biological difference but it applies only to the average man and woman. Individual women can be larger and more muscular than some men. However, culture accentuates this difference as boys and men are encouraged to become muscular and strong while girls and women are usually dissuaded from doing so. It must be admitted that the image of women as small and weak may have helped them as consumers because of the desire to 'protect' them.

In this country the question of strength has traditionally been the reason why women have not been involved in the industry which creates housing – the building industry. Professions such as surveying, valuation and architecture have also remained heavily male dominated, probably because of their association with (and origins in) the building trade. It was suggested in Chapter 9 that the male image of the building trade has affected the fluctuating fortunes of women in housing employment.

This male image of the building trade and associated professions is, however, being challenged. Women have undertaken heavy manual work in building and other industries both in this country and elsewhere. For example, agriculture is often regarded as a woman's job in other communities yet it is physically very hard work. Also there are, and always have been, some jobs in the construction industry which require manual dexterity (often recognised as high in women) rather than brute strength. It is interesting to note that the wearing of trousers rather than skirts seem to free women more easily to do such jobs and such adaptation of fashion is made rapidly when need prevails, for example during wartime. Most of the tasks in housing organisations and politics require stamina rather than physical strength, and there is no evidence that women are lacking in this. Rather the reverse is true.

Women and not men bear children

It is at the childbearing stage that a woman is in the most need of adequate shelter and is least able both financially and physically to provide it for herself. In a patriarchal society this fact is used to reinforce the idea of the woman's dependence on a man. In Britain the State has tended to assume support by a male breadwinner. Only gradually have the needs of unsupported mothers been recognised and to some extent met. The needs of such groups have been largely met by local authority or housing association provision, which is one reason why the policies and procedures of these bodies are of such importance to women.

In the employment market women, when they have children, are removed at a vital stage in their careers if they stay at home for a spell. Recently some action has been taken to keep jobs open for them for some months after childbirth, but there are limitations in this approach which will be discussed later. Those women who have been making a career in politics (especially local politics) do not even have this help.

It is also important when considering childbearing to remember that there are many women, both married and unmarried, who cannot, or do not choose to, have children. As the ability to choose whether or not to have children increases and the social pressures to have children gradually lessen, the number of voluntarily childless women may well increase significantly. There has also been a reduction in the effective duration of childbearing and about 85 per cent of families are complete within 10 years of marriage.[1] Women will therefore be able to return to work earlier and many will wish to do so. This obviously affects both their ability to earn higher incomes and so improve their access to housing and also their availability for housing or political work. Thus even this most biologically based difference is affected by society and culture.

The effect of stereotyped sex roles

The assumption that a woman will marry and form part of a nuclear family, will care for the children and will also care for any needy relatives has had widespread consequences. It has influenced the design of houses and been the reason why the needs of single and 'unconventional' households have been relatively ignored until recent years. On the break up of a relationship the woman is still the partner most likely to be given the care of the children. She is therefore at that point both in greater need of housing and less able to afford it. Responsibility for the care of elderly relatives can also leave a woman at a disadvantage in the housing market.

Since it is assumed in traditional households that women are the home makers a great deal of their time when not at work is spent in domestic activities. Before leaving home, in the lunch hour and after work, the many tasks involved in running a household tend to dominate their so called spare time. Men who are largely free of these responsibilities can be single minded in pursuit of a career or politics after normal working hours. Feminist writers also point out that the role of women is regarded as less important as well as different.

It is, however, worth noting that the ideal of the family played quite an important place in the improvement of housing conditions. Much Victorian literature about housing reform stressed the 'immorality' of bad housing conditions and the impossibility of maintaining a reasonable family life where there was overcrowding or lack of amenities. Unfortunately some of these conditions still exist today, for example the educational disadvantage of children brought up in poor housing conditions is set out clearly in *From Birth to Seven.*[2]

In the field of employment the expectation that women will interrupt their careers to have children has meant that employers tend to assume that they are not as career orientated as men.

Part of the stereotyping of sex roles has been the dogma that there are certain innate differences in intelligence and other psychological attributes between men and women. As we mentioned in Chapter 9, even where differences in behaviour can be established, it is much more difficult to prove whether these are innate or conditioned by society. Maccoby and Jacklin in a recent massive and painstaking survey of the literature on this subject conclude that this distinction does not bear close scrutiny.[3] They state that many of the common beliefs about psychological differences between the sexes are not borne out by the evidence and that there are only a few which are well defined. "Many popular beliefs about the psychological characteristics of the two sexes . . . have proved to have little or no basis in fact . . . A more likely explanation for the perpetuation of 'myths', we believe, is the fact that stereotypes are such powerful things."[4]

As we saw, belief in sex role stereotypes is not confined to men. Feminist writers have often commented that part of the process of socialisation is encouraging girls to 'internalise' such ideas, so that women themselves are doubtful of their own abilities. Society teaches women to see success as something masculine "A successful woman is, therefore, an 'unfeminine' woman, denying her true role as wife and mother."[5]

The logical outcome of stereotyped views is discrimination against women. Though this has now been made illegal in employment the law is weak and has proved difficult to enforce. Shirley Williams argues that discrimination is still one of the powerful factors keeping women out of the House of Commons, "Is it prejudice that keeps women out of Parliament? Yes, a bit. Women candidates are young, attractive and marriageable, or married and likely to have babies, or actually have young children, or are too old to start on the long political ladder. . . ."[6] Thus the effect of these stereotyped views is as powerful where policy is debated as it is in the field of employment.

Different associative styles

Comment has been made at various points on the difference in the ways in which groups of men and women organise themselves (i.e. different 'associative styles'). There is no evidence to indicate whether this is innate or cultural though it seems likely that culture has at least a significant influence.

It has been suggested in a number of places that many women do not seem to like formal organisations and the trappings of power. This idea has a parallel in the study by Vallance of women M.P.s. While indicating that there is no single, simple explanation of why there are so few she claims that it is at least possible that the ritual and ceremonial of the House based on talk rather than action does not necessarily appeal to women "whose experience is largely practical, pragmatic and here and now".[7] Joan Lestor believes that "even women without children are not trying to get into the house in sufficient numbers" inhibited, she thinks, "by the extent to which it is and is seen to be a man's world".[8] And Shirley Williams, explaining that the hours in Parliament were arranged long ago to suit the requirements of lawyers, comments that "the House of Commons remains so influenced by their [lawyers] needs, it will continue to ensure the extreme under-representation of women".[9]

These statements are similar to those of the women members of the Society of Housing Managers who found both the general tone and the style of organisation of the Institute of Housing unfamiliar and uncomfortable when they joined forces. Only the most determined of women will be able to survive being in a 'cultural minority' and women, because of their tradition of being less openly competitive, have less chance in succeeding in the institutions of power. However, it may be that the next generation of women will be more used to formal organisations and may not feel this sense of alienation to the same degree.

Some reasons for the gains and losses

Having looked at some of the underlying causes it will perhaps be easier to see why change has been more beneficial to women in the field of access to housing than in politics and employment. It is appropriate to examine the various factors which bring about social change and see how they have operated differently in each case. In Chapter 4 we quoted the George and Wilding argument that before action is taken on a social problem it must pose a problem for the whole of society and the condition must be one which is capable of improvement. How far do these apply to access and influence in housing?

Research is one of the ways in which social problems are identified and measured. It has been instrumental in helping to identify the problems of women as consumers, as was noted in Chapter 4 – though possibly direct social action has been as powerful. It is interesting to note that some of the leading researchers in this field are women. Valerie Karn, Clare Ungerson and Jan Pahl are all experts in their particular spheres. The majority of social researchers working in this area within the Department of the Environment are also women.

As far as women in housing employment is concerned, virtually no specific research has been done previously although one or two individuals have tried to draw attention to the problem.[10] We see our own attempt to research this field as only a beginning and hope that others will do more detailed work. On the other hand there has by now been a considerable amount of general research identifying the disadvantages of women in employment, especially at professional or managerial levels. So far this seems also to have had little effect.

In the field of policy making, particularly at a local level, there has been substantial general research but very little directly related to housing. The research by the Maud and Robinson committees identified some of the factors affecting women's participation in local politics and this has been supplemented by more recent studies of women in local politics[11] and in Parliament. This important research has as yet, however, not led to much improvement in the position of women.

Setting out the facts makes little impact without publicity and it is here that *the media* have an important role. But people in need, whether homeless unmarried mothers, overcrowded families or old people in unsuitable accommodation are much more photogenic and newsworthy than statements about the small number of women M.P.s, chairmen of committees and policy makers in housing organisations. Although some newspapers and journals do give some space, the subject only rarely gets an airing on the most powerful medium of television. Also the media in many cases help to perpetuate sexual stereotypes, particularly in advertising. It must also be admitted that far more people are affected by the problem as 'consumers'. The lack of women in policy making is not such a 'visible' issue.

Individuals have traditionally played a major part in achieving changes in social policy. In recent years women have taken on this role as spokesmen for vulnerable groups. Erin Pizzey for battered women, Margaret Bramall for single parent families and Heather McKenzie for single women and their dependants have spoken up forcibly on behalf of particular groups. In housing employment only a small number of the remarkable women who were pioneers have been mentioned. Yet at one stage their influence seemed to have been lost without trace. Similarly the early women pioneers in politics did not lead on to any substantial growth in the number of women influential in politics. Elizabeth Vallance argues that the same will apply to the election of the first woman Prime Minister – it will not necessarily lead to more women participating in politics.

Pressure groups usually have a part in identifying social problems, drawing attention to them, and pressing for action. Chapter 10 demonstrated the curious fact that although women may be involved at grass roots level in the pressure groups concerned with housing they are not involved in the leadership. Such groups often lay great stress on the suffering caused to women and children by bad housing and they have helped to keep the general housing problems in the front of public attention. The groups more closely concerned with women's issues have been the National Council for One Parent Families, the Joint Finer Action Group, the National Women's Aid Federation and the National Council for the Single Woman and her Dependants. The ones in which women have played the most prominent part have been the all women's organisations like N.W.A.F. which has been successful in drawing attention to, and getting some action on, what was at one time a very hidden social problem. It is relevant to note that this Federation works very much on a local, devolved and informal basis thus again showing the differences in associative style. Chapter 6 showed how the Society of Women Housing Managers acted as a pressure group for women in housing employment and also took an interest, for example, in the housing of single women. After World War Two, and particularly after the admission of men, it was no longer possible for it to carry out this role.

Many of the senior women housing managers interviewed felt a reluctance to be identified with women's issues, especially when this was taken to mean, for example, special knowledge about the siting of sink units. Like the women M.P.s many would prefer to be regarded as people doing a good job rather than as 'women'. On the other hand their very scarcity makes them stand out as such.

Pressure groups do not seem to have been very influential in regard to women in politics since the 1930s. The women M.P.s have mixed views about being associated with women's issues or acting in any way as a concerted group. Elizabeth Vallance shows there has been a swing first of all away from being identified with women's issues and then slowly back to a growing realisation that this may, on occasion, be needed. In fact the nearest thing to concerted bi-party action has been seen in the recent struggles over abortion law reform.

The varying attitudes of those within the *Women's Movement* are of interest. It must, however, be remembered that many women are outside this movement and can feel alienated by the aggressive stance taken by some feminists. Quite clearly it has been relatively easy to marshall the support of considerable sections of the women's movement to help battered women both by legislation and direct provision. Similarly most women in the movement support efforts to eliminate the remaining legal and economic disadvantages which face women in obtaining housing. However the position regarding women in employment and politics is somewhat more complicated. The 'women's rights' and equal rights campaigns arose at the earlier stages of the women's movement. To some extent they were criticised as helping only those women who were already relatively advantaged and were too limited in accepting many of the male defined values of society.

Another factor is that, as in many minority and radical groups, there is a distrust of those who are too successful. To a certain extent this may be justified. Writers have identified what they call the 'Queen Bee' syndrome. They say that these are "successful professionals in a man's world" and women who tend to be anti-feminist. "Women who try to keep other women down even though they are in a position to advance women's cause." Various reasons are given for this, for example, that such people have been co-opted by the establishment and knowing their position is somewhat precarious they may tend not to adopt a militant stance. This may be a way of excluding competition from other women. In addition if the 'Queen Bee' has had to overcome many obstacles to obtain her position she may feel that others should endure the same fight. Summing up she is someone who has little to gain from a change in the status quo. While this presents a problem for other women there is said to be evidence that the incidence of this syndrome is decreasing.[12]

Some sections of the women's movement have as an integral part of their philosophy the adoption of forms of organisation reflecting some of the traditional female values rather than the traditional male values. Thus there is an emphasis on equality, on co-operation as opposed to competition, on unstructured communal organisation rather than hierarchy. Women who have made their way in the present structures may be seen to have adopted male values in order to do so. Similar conflicts have arisen in the past in community and grass roots activity where those who become articulate are gradually pushed into organisations and local politics. In learning to manipulate the machine they themselves are taken over by it.

The inherent difficulty in resolving this conflict is nicely illustrated in housing. It could be argued that in housing the 'women's liberation' values are better expressed in the formation of women's co-operatives and in the running of women's aid than in pushing for opportunities for individual women to reach the top of the existing male dominated and hierarchical housing organisations. However, in order for co-operatives or refuges to come into being they may have to gain the approval of the local authority or of the Housing Corporation where men are in most senior positions. Thus the issue of power faces the women's movement with a difficult problem and makes it more divided and uncertain about what to do on the employment issue. Should the answer lie in attempting to dismantle or undermine the existing hierarchical structures rather than penetrating them? Or could the two go on simultaneously?

The Equal Opportunities Commission is less ambiguous in its relationship to both the issues discussed here. It has already shown some interest in the position of women in the housing market and a general interest in women in employment. Although the law itself is still not sufficiently strong, there has been criticism of the E.O.C.'s failure to pursue the issue of employment more vigorously. Some unions are beginning to take more action on behalf of their women members on a national and local basis and this includes the National and Local Government Officers Association (N.A.L.G.O.), the body to which most non-manual housing staff belong. So far some local authorities have adopted declared Equal Opportunities policies and more generous provision, e.g. for maternity leave, than the law compels. However, as was shown earlier, this approach tends to be modelled on women following the career patterns of men, rather than tackling the more difficult question of attitudes.

But where there has been action, it is interesting to note that *external influences* seem to have had just as much impact as the more amorphous threat to the values of society or, indeed, as any overt desire for action. Two examples are the influence of economic factors and the effect of war. On economic grounds, for instance, it could be held that one reason for the greater independent housing provision for the elderly and for single parent families is that the cost of institutional care for old people (or in the case of single parent families, their children) is likely to be higher.

The effect of wars has been a recurrent topic in our consideration of the changing role of women in the various spheres. Described recently as 'the big break-through' the First World War helped to explode the myth that certain jobs were 'unfeminine'. It was responsible for the first major move of women housing managers into public employment. Due to public pressure many women had to give up their jobs at the end of the war but World War Two gave them the chance to work again and to take on positions of leadership. We saw in Chapter 10 that women who were street wardens became used to taking a lead in local affairs. History has shown once again that directly the war or similar emergency is over then there is a tendency for society to revert to its former values.

But even if the advances made in wartime have not been totally sustained the gradual advance of women overall in paid labour cannot be ignored. Although women are concentrated in lower grade work and in certain industries, usually earning far less than men, the fact that more women can now support themselves economically is probably one of the most important forces for change. Greater economic independence should lead to greater independence of thought and action. In the long run, so long as we have a 'democratic' society, the power of women, now the majority of the population, at the ballot box will not be able to be ignored.

One of the most interesting comparisons to make is to consider the extent to which women's disadvantages in access to housing and their influence in housing challenge society's values or otherwise. Where women are suffering from disadvantage in housing they are clearly challenging the 'residual conscience' of society. Particularly if children are involved, policy makers are aware that to allow the continuance of bad housing conditions, especially overcrowding, insecurity and homelessness, is merely to store up trouble for the future. Unfortunately, the 'conscience' of society over bad housing has always had to fight a running battle with political values about the ownership of property and with ideas about the 'deserving' and the 'undeserving' poor.

The pressure for women to be more involved in policy decisions about housing cannot appeal to the same kind of charitable impulse. To some extent it is in conflict with society's values. The attitude of much of society is still that a woman's place is in the home, and is against improving conditions or altering sex roles so that she can get out more easily. Increasing the involvement of women outside the home is seen as a threat to these values.

However, challenging the seat of power is bound to be a difficult job. It began over one hundred years ago when women got the vote. The very lack of progress so far indicates that those entrenched in power do not give it up easily. This indeed is probably the one most important reason why women have made much less progress in influence than in access to housing – because in seeking to become senior staff, chairmen of committees or M.P.s they are seeking to share in the power structure which governs housing.

The way forward

Attitudes

It may seem a cliché, in a book about women, to talk about changes in attitudes. Nevertheless, these cannot be ignored. The most powerful factor in maintaining (or supporting) the disadvantages which women still suffer in obtaining housing, or in influencing its provision, is the attitude which assumes that every woman has certain stereotyped characteristics and that she has a predetermined role within the nuclear family.

As far as access to housing is concerned there is still room for improvement, even though attitudes are better than they were. For instance single mothers do not face quite the same stigma that they once did, although some still feel that there is a degree of social stigma attached to their position which makes it difficult for them to get appropriate housing and causes them to be regarded as 'a problem'. There may be room for change in the attitudes of housing staff. The Housing Services Advisory Group has said "It would be more appropriate for housing staff to think 'there but for the Grace of God go I, or, more likely, my wife and children or my daughter and her children' than to regard them as less deserving members of society."[13] In a wider sense, so long as housing staff are influenced by stereotyped sex roles and the idealisation of the nuclear family, housing organisations will fail to encourage policies of equal opportunities and equality of access to housing. This is particularly likely in the case of unconventional households.

Changes in the law, as has been seen, have improved access to housing and have attempted to improve employment prospects for women. But as the White Paper *Equality for Women* argued "In dealing with an issue of this kind there is a role, limited but indispensable, to be played by legislation. There is much that Government can do by example, beyond this there are wide areas in which the government itself can do little. Hence it must invite individual men and women to give effect to the spirit of the law rather than their letter, and to establish as a social reality the equality of opportunity to which women are entitled."[14] An example of this is discrimination in employment which is notoriously hard to prove. While some employers continue to hold the view that women's place is in the home and to doubt women's ability to hold down certain types of jobs the law clearly has only limited use as a weapon.

The attitudes of society also often lead to women's aspirations being limited, as numerous studies have shown. The Department of Employment (D.E.P.) in *Women and Work: a review* pointed out that the career and job chances of females tend to be much narrower than those of men and boys. They said "Most women are prepared to seek work within the conventional areas. Women with domestic responsibilities are further constrained by the need to find work that is compatible with their domestic role."[15]

But role models can help to widen women's horizons and also help change the attitudes of society. The early pioneers in housing management provided many other women with examples of what could be achieved. Tessa Blackstone, charting the inroads women have made into higher education, considers that in a situation where there are very few women the role model of a successful woman is important.[16] But she goes on to admit however that few of the women scientists who have reached the top "are able to provide a model of the successful combination of marriage, family and a brilliant career".

This is not to suggest that women should simply take over the aspirations of men. One of the interesting findings of the P.E.P. report *Women and Top Jobs: The Next Move* was that women were more likely than men to have a wide range of life aims.[17] They were less likely to focus ruthlessly on the achievement of top posts or of great power and wealth. Perhaps men could find enrichment from a greater variety of interests and aims. In later sections some of the practical implications of such a philosophy will be discussed.

Because of the importance of stereotypes the efforts of all those groups such as Women in the Media, Women in Education and AFFIRM (Alliance for Fair Images and Representation in the Media) which seek to break down sexual stereotypes are useful. But there is a need to do this work within housing also. For example the use of stereotypes which are still current, in architecture and planning, particularly concepts like 'head of household' with its patriarchal overtones, should not be continued into the 1980s.

Sharing the caring

One move towards breaking down the sexual stereotypes is the gradual advance towards sharing the burden of 'caring' more equally. At the moment this sharing seems only to occur in exceptional cases. Nickie Fonda and Cary Cooper in an article in *The Guardian* 'Working Women into the System' identify two sorts of people who seem to be able to combine motherhood and working: the 'superwoman' who can organise her life in such a way as to cope and the woman who has what they term a "special breed of husband".[18] He is the one who encourages his wife and takes over "a significant portion of the child care and domestic responsibilities". This sort of woman seems to do well in whatever sphere she chooses and is unlikely to figure in one of the disadvantaged groups.

What is of greater concern is the majority of women who are not so fortunate. The woman with an unsupportive husband, or who is not married, has no one to encourage her or share the domestic responsibilities. And often women who care for an elderly relative are worse off. Even studying can prove a virtual impossibility under such circumstances.[19] A change in attitudes enabling greater equality between men and women is insufficient without some more practical action. *Sharing the caring* is how we would sum up this change. Instead of the automatic assumption that women will do all the caring, whether it is for children or elderly relatives, a more equal solution is for this task to be shared. For society benefits if personal care is given. While crêches, day nurseries, nursery schools for children and day centres for the elderly all have their part to play, what many dependent relatives really need, at least for some of the time, is to be looked after in a personal way preferably in their own home. As Lyn Owen says in a review of the Equal Opportunities Commission report, *I want to work, but what about the kids?*, parents have voted with their feet and most have opted either to stay at home or for participatory playgroups or child minders.[20] If the care of young children were as valued in our society as is the running of a large organisation, then the man or woman who has taken time off from their career to do this would not be so heavily penalised in terms of career structure as they are at the moment. If a more flexible view was taken of the role of women in society they would not be forced either to conform to the traditional female role or to adopt the traditional male role. Nor would appointing bodies automatically assume, as many now do, that women will leave their career through marriage and children.

In Sweden, where many of the practical measures so often advocated have been carried out, it is beginning to be recognised that more fundamental changes must go with them. Olof Palme, ex Prime Minister of Sweden, said "The new role of the man implies that he must reduce his contributions in working life – and maybe also in politics – during the period when he has small children. This is what women always had to do alone earlier . . . we could manage this loss in production if we can instead stimulate women to make increased contributions in this area."[21]

In Soviet Russia, although women are still as a whole in lower paid jobs, far more progress has been made in some professions (for example over 50 per cent of doctors are women). Yet these women have had to bear the whole load of the 'dual burden' of family and career. Feminists here are also beginning to say that it is essential that this caring task should be more evenly spread.[22]

Young and Willmott pointed out in *The Symmetrical Family* that men and women are now beginning to share the various roles in a family.[23] And Nickie Fonda and Cary Cooper have shown that men are coming to terms with dual career families.[24] They say that one sign of this is the increasing reluctance of men to move to another part of the country unless their wives can also find suitable employment there.

Men, too, may gain from this sharing and welcome the chance to spend more time with their families. And women must accept that, if a marriage breaks down, it will sometimes be right for the man to bring up the children.

Before men and women can more equally share in the caring for dependants, whether children or the aged, one other thing is essential – paid work must be more evenly distributed.

Sharing the work

A significant number of studies have now shown that there are certain practical steps which can be taken even within the existing employment system, both to help women get better jobs in the first instance and to help them carry on working when they have young children. A certain amount has already been done in the provision of maternity leave and the legal requirement to keep jobs open for women returning to work after childbearing. But a number of other measures would help. These include encouraging schoolgirls to raise their horizons and to participate more fully in further education and training, and making such opportunities more available to them. For women with children, whether married or unmarried, the provision of crêches, play centres for after school hours, the availability of part time work and training for 're-entry' after a period at home are all known to be helpful. These changes would help women generally in terms of access to housing through increasing their incomes. They would help more single parents to live independently, and would also help those women employed in the housing service.

In housing, a more determined attempt to monitor the 'wastage' from housing work of qualified women who marry and have children would be useful. At the moment nothing is known about these women, other than that the Institute statistics indicate that there is probably a loss. Since 35 per cent of those now qualifying are women, it is surely worth finding out the extent of that 'wastage', and seeing what can be done to encourage their return to work. Otherwise the housing service is not getting the benefit of the training provided. Attempts have been made to study this subject in other professions such as education and social work. One significant factor which has been identified is that the provision of part time work makes the re-entry of women with children easier. Once they have returned in this way they are likely to move gradually to full time work. Such posts are now available in social work at reasonably senior levels. The provision of courses or training specifically for re-entry is also helpful.

Training would also be useful for non-qualified women who either are currently employed in housing or wish to take up this work. Staff who are mature and have been through some of their own 'life crises' are well equipped for some of the stressful jobs in housing. At the moment, unqualified women probably stand little opportunity of moving out of lower paid jobs, though the "Housing Staff" study showed that there was interest in further training opportunities.

Such measures are likely to be particularly important in the housing service over the next few years, since both social and general historical trends seem to indicate that the number of staff may not grow, but rather may decline, while the proportion of qualified staff desired may increase. Since women at the moment comprise most of the lower grade staff it is they who will lose their jobs in the process, making the present imbalance even more pronounced.

The Local Government Operational Research Unit is currently investigating ways of improving women's career opportunities in local government. This includes both the identification of women's career problems and the production and testing of briefing materials to be used in presenting women's employment issues to local authority staff. Among observations they make on a current study in a planning department are:

" – the concentration of professional women in 'research' type jobs which tend not to lead to line management.

– the absence of a career structure [. . .] for those (mainly women) in administrative posts.

The degree to which women were planning for a 'third career' after an expected 'second career' of child rearing also seemed of significance."[25]

These are interesting findings in view of the earlier discussion of housing employment and it is to be hoped that the study will lead to some positive improvements.

The concept of a 'third career' leads to another important way of sharing the work – more equal distribution of work between the age groups. Parents who have chosen to break their careers to look after their children may well return to their former occupation or even to a new career with renewed energy and the ability to fill a demanding post. The existing career pattern, depending on early promotion, does not allow for this. On the other hand, men or women who have achieved success by middle age, and find themselves in extremely stressful posts by their late fifties and early sixties, might welcome some reduction of pressure through a move to less full time work.

Better options for a more gradual 'winding down' at the pre-retirement stage is something which those concerned with the care of the elderly have been advocating for some time. Flexible rather than rigid ways of looking at career structures could help both men and women. Such changes in work patterns may seem rather idealistic. However, there are changes at present taking place both in industry and commerce which make such a reconsideration of values more appropriate.

For many years 'futurists' have been forecasting that the time would come when work would be a privilege and the problem would be what to do with leisure. With the rapid progress of the microchip and other similar technological advances this time has now arrived. Unfortunately society at the moment is failing to face up to the situation and there are signs that the changes may worsen the position of women unless countervailing action is taken. It is the more routine jobs such as clerical work and assembling, which women often do, which will disappear. Also, when jobs are scarce, history shows that there is a tendency to revert to the view that it is more important to employ a man because he is head of the household. Women are then driven back into the home. Many people feel that signs of such a reversal in attitudes are already present.

If, instead of attempting to reverse the social revolution of the last few years, a determined effort was made to use these changes positively, great benefit could be gained. The biggest step towards sharing the caring and sharing the work would be shorter working hours – or staggered days of work for both men and women. Another option is one suggested by Mia Kellmer Pringle. This is that parenting should be a shared task which would involve "rotating the home-making role, each parent in turn undertaking it for say, a three or four year period".[26] Idealistic? Yes, it is, but surely it is a more appropriate solution for the 21st century than trying to push the clock back and confine women to a narrow domestic role. Possibly this is the single most important aim which women should now be pursuing.

Affirmative action

To some extent in the U.S.A. equal opportunities policies have been pursued in a more dynamic way by the use of 'positive discrimination' or 'affirmative action' (i.e. efforts to ensure that disadvantaged groups are properly represented in all the places of influence). Such policies have come in for much criticism and are not acceptable to all women.

As far as housing is concerned the government in the United States set up a Women's Policy and Program Division in 1976 to concentrate on 'the needs and concerns of women consumers and women providers outside of H.U.D.' (Department of Housing and Urban Development, which is the central government body dealing with housing.) Equal opportunities within H.U.D. were dealt with by another section.[27] Studies had shown that women were either largely ignored or actively discriminated against in local planning and housing activities and that women were particularly affected by the lack of low income housing. There was also concern about the lack of women in significant numbers and at significant decision making levels in construction, planning and design, house management and other related careers. This is a very familiar picture. But the establishment of the 'Women's Office' aimed to overcome these difficulties in a variety of ways, working closely with women's groups and community organisations. Could this be a pattern that should be followed in Britain?

Even if such specific action would not be acceptable, at the very least pressure needs to be brought to bear on public employers in housing to pursue declared Equal Opportunities Policies, to make sure that discrimination is not unintentionally built in to selection for training or appointment, or in procedures for allocation and management. The Institute of Housing could encourage housing employers to do this. It could also carry out measures specifically to monitor the participation and employment of qualified women.

One immediate and inexpensive step which central and local government could take would be to use their powers of co-option to redress the sex imbalance on so many bodies concerned with housing. This need not mean calling on people who are inexperienced but the recognition that women who have interrupted or delayed their careers because of children may have a great deal to offer in terms of maturity and wide experience. Some attention is being paid to this. For example the Commons Select Committee on the Treasury and the Civil Service has criticised the way in which the people who fill the 25,000 public appointments under the patronage of Ministers are chosen. A *maximum* of 20 per cent of these are women.[28]

In general, affirmative action could be taken by the organisations concerned becoming more aware of the position of women and their presence or absence in places of influence. It is interesting to note that this issue has already been raised in one housing pressure group – the Cyrenians (who are concerned with the single homeless). An article by one of their members points out that "Cyrenians is one more place where it is mostly men", and suggests that if any organisations in this field are to continue to be radical they will have to "confront the sexism, subtle and not so subtle, in their organisation, practice, aims and ideals".[29] This could be a good objective for all the organisations involved.

Changes in housing organisations

We have already pointed out that two changes in housing organisations seemed to make their climate less favourable to women in the 1950s and 60s. These were the growth of the large organisations and the retreat from the welfare role. However current changes could reverse both of these directions.

Large housing organisations have been under attack because of their impersonal nature and the difficulty of management on such a large scale. Many are seeing what they can do to devolve their responsibilities on to a local level. At the moment this may be rather a paper exercise but in the future it could become more of a reality. Certainly there is no longer quite such a blanket assumption that 'big is beautiful' as there was in the 50s and 60s. There is more experimentation with co-operatives and other forms of smaller local organisations. Could the large organisations become the dinosaurs of housing? Small organisations can find it easier to work in the less hierarchical way which women seem to find more congenial. Such organisations may also be more responsive to the needs of women as clients.

Current policies may mean that public housing will assume a more residual and welfare role. Because of the association of women with the caring role this may also work in favour of increasing their employment. However, this kind of role may be unwelcome and also has its own dangers. In the newer and larger housing associations, for example, women have complained that they are largely confined to the 'ghetto' of management and welfare while men predominate in the more prestigeous functions such as development. Since it is the development function which deals with the form and location of what is to be built, this sexual division of work within housing organisations benefits neither the employed women nor women as consumers.

Thus, changes in the nature of housing organisations have the potential for improving women's access and influence in housing but will only do so if the opportunity is seized.

Advice and support for women

It was noted in the history of the Society of Women Housing managers that not only did the senior members of the Society provide role models but the Society as a whole provided a valuable social support for women and helped them to proceed with their chosen career. This principle of women helping women is one which is very much in tune with the modern women's movement. It has been at the cornerstone of the work of Women's Aid Centres. Rights of Women are now trying more actively to provide housing advice for women. One of the advantages of women giving advice to other women is that in learning how to give advice women begin to learn more about how the system works and to understand what needs to be changed within it. A separate professional body is no longer what women want but supportive networks within the existing structures can be important. Thus the Feminist Architecture Group, Women and Housing, Women in the Civil Service and Women in Design have already started to fulfil this role. Groups of this type may have as their predominating interest the level of service provided or availability of employment. Such informal bodies can help those women who feel less confident to penetrate the 'male dominated club' of established professions or their senior membership. While pressing for a better deal and change in policies they can also fulfil a valuable role in acting as a support group for individuals. Perhaps, as these groups emerge in the occupations concerned with housing, planning and building, it may be possible to see more informal links made between them so that valuable experience can be exchanged. They may also feel the need for more action in terms of career advice for girls.

Better access to housing and more understanding of how housing problems affect women
The earlier part of this book showed very clearly how women predominated in certain 'disadvantaged groups'. Detailed suggestions were made in Chapter 4 about some of the changes which might be made to improve women's access to housing. Many of the changes suggested involve measures which would enable women to find their way better in the existing system – closer links between departments, better advice and the removal of discriminatory practices, particularly in the public sector. Some changes in provision would help too, such as more small homes, special types of accommodation in certain limited cases and easier transfers and exchanges.

Suggestions were also made about measures which would give greater security and better conditions in an existing tenure and others which would make it easier to change from one tenure to another. Finally the point was made that while many women are concerned simply about getting access to ordinary housing, some of the newer kinds of tenure (i.e. equity sharing or co-operatives) may offer positive advantages.

Many of the measures which would help women are those which would help most people seeking accommodation, that is better provision of housing for those in need. It has been argued that current policies seem to be moving away from this and housing is taking a 'back seat' as a social priority. Unfortunately, the effects of such policies tend to show up only gradually, but the long cycle of building development is such that once a housing crisis has been allowed to occur it is many years before the situation can be improved. As the competition for housing increases it is those who are at a disadvantage who suffer and the majority of these will be women. There is therefore an urgent need to make women more knowledgeable and more aware of the effect of housing policies.

Those seeking information about almost any aspect of the subject covered in this book will come up against major problems of lack of information. It seems strange that so little data on housing is analysed on a sex basis. One reason may be that women are 'hidden', as for example when a man is head of household. But for single person households it is often easier to obtain a breakdown according to ethnic origin or age than it is on sex. Greater attention to the importance of distinguishing between male and females over such things

144

as successful and unsuccessful applicants for mortgages or people in top jobs would help to pinpoint more accurately the position of women.

Conclusions

It is easy to blame other people and external factors for women's relatively poor position in housing. While some of this is justified an internal change is needed as much as anything. As Elizabeth Vallance has said, "women will be relegated to the sidelines and the support systems in party as in factory and office, while they themselves predominantly accept this as their appropriate role".[30] Women are after all in the majority in the country and at the ballot box. If Britain follows trends in the U.S.A. they may even end up controlling substantial proportions of the country's wealth. If women decide that they no longer want a society which relegates them to the kitchen sink or to the strain of doing two jobs at once then it is up to them to change this.

If housing is important to women, should the major decisions about it be left to men?

References

1. M. Britton. 'Women at Work', *Population Trends*, No. 2, Winter 1975, pp. 22–25.
2. R. Davie, M. Butler and H. Goldstein. *From Birth to Seven*, Longman in association with the National Children's Bureau, 1972, p. 57.
3. E. E. Maccoby and C. N. Jacklin. *The Psychology of Sex Differences*, Oxford University Press, 1975, p. 363.
4. *Ibid.* p. 355. And D.E.P. in Manpower Paper: *Women and Work: Sex differences and society*, H.M.S.O., 1974, p. 3 note the effect of differences on environment.
5. J. Morrison (ed.). 'Society Today: Woman's role', *New Society*, 23.11.78, p. iii.
6. S. Williams. 'Housebound', *The Guardian*, 30.10.79.
7. E. Vallance. *Women in the House*, Athlone Press, 1979, p. 22.
8. Joan Lestor quoted by E. Vallance. 'The hand that rocks the cradle lacks the power in politics', *The Guardian*, 31.10.79.
9. S. Williams. *op. cit.*
10. For example, P. Gallagher. *Women in Housing* – paper to the Institute of Housing Study Group Conference, 1975. And M. E. H. Smith, letter to *Housing*, November, 1973, p. 54.
11. S. Bristow. 'Women Councillors', *County Councils Gazette*, May, November and December 1978.
12. J. S. Hyde and B. G. Rosenberg. *Half the Human Experience*. D. C. Heath and Co., Lexington, U.S.A., 1976, Ch. 5.
13. D.O.E. Housing Services Advisory Group, *The Housing of One-Parent Families*, H.M.S.O., 1978, p. 8.
14. Home Office, *Equality for Women*, Cmnd 5724, H.M.S.O., 1974, p. 1.
15. D.E.P. Manpower Papers, No. 11, *Women and Work: a review*, H.M.S.O., 1975, p. 58.
16. T. Blackstone. 'Success or failure?', *The Times Higher Education Supplement*, 8.9.78.
17. M. Fogarty with R. and R. Rapoport. *Women and Top Jobs: The Next Move*, P.E.P., 1972.
18. N. Fonda and C. Cooper. 'Working Women into the System', *The Guardian*, 25.8.77.
19. P. Kirk. 'Owing to a family crisis', *New Society*, 17.1.80, pp. 119–120.
20. L. Owen. 'Opportunities Knocked', *The Observer*, 15.10.78.
21. O. Palme quoted in E. Vallance. *op. cit.* p. 162.
22. N. Hodson. 'Breakthrough in Russia', *Spare Rib*, March, 1980, p. 55.
23. M. Young and P. Willmott. *The Symmetrical Family*, Routledge & Kegan Paul 1973.
24. N. Fonda and C. Cooper, *op. cit.*
25. Local Government Operational Research Unit. *Progress Newsletter*, No. 2, January, 1980.

26. M. Kellmer Pringle. 'Giving mothering back its dignity', *Community Care*, 23.8.78, pp. 26–28.
27. A. Skinner. 'Women Consumers, Women Professionals', National Association of Housing and Redevelopment Officials, *Journal of Housing*, May, 1978, Vol. 35, No. 5.
28. *The Guardian*, 6.2.80.
29. M. Titley. *Rough Justice*, Autumn 1979.
30. E. Vallance. *op. cit.*, p. 177.

Appendix: Sources of the Data

Access to housing

Chapters 2–4 are drawn mainly from published sources of information. These include official statistics (e.g. *Social Trends, The General Household Survey*), reports (e.g. the Cullingworth report *Council Housing Purposes, Procedures and Priorities*, the Finer report *One-Parent Families*) and Government Consultation Papers (e.g. D.H.S.S. *A Happier Old Age*, D.O.E. *Housing Policy*). But it also draws heavily on research produced by organisations such as the Equal Opportunities Commission, the National Council for the Single Woman and her Dependants, Child Poverty Action Group, Shelter Housing Aid Centre and the National Women's Aid Federation.

Women in the housing service

Statistics on women members of the Institute of Housing

These statistics were taken from Institute year books and publications. The main disadvantage of using these figures is that Institute membership may not be a reliable guide in estimating the numbers of qualified men and women in employment. Membership of the Institute is not compulsory, nor usually necessary for employment, once a person has qualified. Thus if for any reason employed women are less likely to continue their membership after qualification than employed men these figures may misrepresent the balance. As we have seen there are historical reasons why women might feel more alienated from the Institute than men and thus fail to continue membership, though there is no factual evidence to support this view.

However, much of the discussion centres round movement in the membership of the Institute over a 12 year period and it is assumed that the dropout rate remained reasonably consistent over the period. Confidence in this interpretation of the figures is increased by the fact that the data on students qualifying, on membership of the council (which does cover the whole population concerned) and on membership of the National Federation Council (which is taken from an entirely separate source) all seem to show a similar pattern.

It would be more satisfactory to have accurate information about the relative 'wastage' rates of qualified men and women. Unfortunately so far it has not been possible to obtain funds for such a survey.

The Interviews

As part of a historical study of the development of the Society and its unification with the Institute interviews were requested with all the members of the committee which dealt with unification who could still be contacted. Interviews were carried out according to a semi-structured format, tape recorded and transcribed. Interviews were obtained with all eight women who represented the Society. Of the five members from the Institute who were still alive (four men and one woman) four gave interviews and one felt unable to give a full interview because of age but did provide some brief details. Material from these interviews is used in the unattributed quotations. Where necessary members are identified by means of their former membership, i.e. 'Society' or 'Institute' interviewee. Quotations sometimes have detail removed to preserve confidentiality. Interviews were also carried out with certain historical or 'key informants'. Where material from these is used it is identified.

Records of the Society and the Institute

Apart from the interviews the main source of information on the history of the Society and the Institute were their annual reports, year books and journals. In particular, the Minutes of the Society which are in existence back to 1933 provide a more qualitative view of what went on. Thanks are due to the Institute and to the Housing Centre Trust for allowing access to these records. As the records are not complete several individuals donated or lent their copies of reports or journals and their help is gratefully acknowledged.

The Education and Training for Housing Work Project

One source of information for the study of women employed in housing work was the Education and Training for Housing Work Project, financed by the Department of the Environment and carried out at The City University from 1975–77. In the first part of this research 288 of the 403 local authorities completed a questionnaire on work and staff in housing departments. Information was obtained about 26,694 staff. Figures for staff of registered housing associations were obtained from Housing Corporation records and from these national figures were estimated. Six local authority housing departments and six housing associations allowed the researchers to carry out detailed studies of their structures, procedures and jobs. Though the departments were chosen to reflect the different types of local authority they were not a random sample. The associations were deliberately chosen to represent the larger ones with paid staff. The main results were published in *Housing Work*.

In these 12 organisations a "Staff Study" was carried out. In each organisation information about the age, grade and sex of all staff was obtained from records and more detailed information obtained from a stratified sample of 795 staff. The main results of this study were published in *Housing Staff* and the limitations of the methods are discussed in Appendix 2 of that report. A small amount of information has also been taken from the report on *Training for Housing Work* produced by the Project.

Councillors, M.P.s, and pressure groups

The main sources of general information about councillors were the research done on a national scale for the Maud Committee *Management of Local Government* in 1964 and for the Robinson Committee *Report of the Inquiry into the system of remuneration of members of local authorities* in 1976. (See also references 1 and 2 of Chapter 10.) Additionally data was obtained from Stephen Bristow's study of women councillors in 1977 and a study by the Greater London Group at the London School of Economics of some London Boroughs 1968–73. (See also reference 6 of Chapter 10.) There was no study of women as chairmen of committees but information about the names of the chairmen of the major committees of all the local authorities was given in the *Municipal Year Book* for the first time in 1977. The 1977 Year Book gave the 1976 figures based on returns from 342 of the 369 District Councils, all the 34 London authorities and 51 of the 53 County Councils in England and Wales. The 1978 Year Book gave the 1977 figures for all local authorities.

Names of women M.P.s and Ministers were obtained from a number of sources. These were Dame Evelyn Sharp's *The Ministry of Housing and Local Government* (1969) Appendix 1, Hansard's Annual Listings of Ministers of State and the Conservative Party's *Women in Politics* (1971 and revised 1980). The Public Information Offices of the House of Commons and the House of Lords were also consulted and produced helpful information. For the members of Advisory Committees there were three sources – the reports of the Central Housing Advisory Committee 1935–1975, published reports of the five ad hoc national committees concerned with housing 1965–75 and the published reports of the New Town Commissions or Development Corporations. *The Guardian Directory of Pressure Groups and Representative Associations* was used to obtain the names of key people (mainly staff but also in some cases members of the governing body) to see how many were women.

Fuller details of the reports and books referred to are given in the appropriate chapters.

SELECT BIBLIOGRAPHY

J. Buckle. *Work and Housing of Impaired Persons in Great Britain*, H.M.S.O., 1971.
Civil Service Department. Management Studies, No. 3, *The Employment of Woman in the Civil Service*, H.M.S.O., 1971.
M. Constable. *Tied Accommodation*, Shelter, 1974.
A. Coote and T. Gill. *Battered Women and the New Law*, Interaction Inprint and National Council for Civil Liberties, 1979.
L. Davidson and L. K. Gordon. *The Sociology of Gender*, Rand, McNally College Publishing Co., U.S.A., 1979.
D.E.P. Manpower Papers, H.M.S.O.:
No. 9 *Women and Work: a Statistical Survey*, 1974.
No. 10 *Women and Work: Sex Differences and Society*, 1974.
No. 11 *Women and Work: a Review*, 1975.
D.O.E. Circular, *Housing for One-Parent Families* (D.O.E. 78/77 and W.O. 123/77), H.M.S.O., 1977.
D.O.E. *One-Parent Families: a Guide to Housing Aid*, D.O.E., 1978.
D.O.E. *The Housing of One-Parent Families*, Housing Services Advisory Group, D.O.E., 1978.
D.O.E. Circular, *Sex Discrimination Act 1975, Provisions Affecting Local Government* (D.O.E. 1/78 and W.O. 3/78), H.M.S.O. 1978.
D.H.S.S. *Report of the Committee on One-Parent Families* (the Finer report), Cmnd. 5629, Volume 1 The Report, Volume 2 Appendices, H.M.S.O., 1974.
Education and Training for Housing Work Project. *Housing Work* and *Housing Staff*, The City University, 1977.
E. Durkin. *Hostels for the Mentally Disordered*, Young Fabian Pamphlet, 24, Fabian Society, 1971.
E.O.C. *'It's not your business, it's how the Society works'*, a report of a survey carried out by the Consumers Association Survey Unit, E.O.C., 1978.
M. Fogarty, A. J. Allen, I. Allen and P. Walters. *Women in Top Jobs*, P.E.P., and Allen and Unwin, 1971.
M. Fogarty with R. and R. Rapoport. *Women and Top Jobs: the Next Move*, P.E.P., 1972.
W. T. Hill. *Octavia Hill*, Hutchinson, 1956.
J. S. Hyde and B. G. Rosenberg. *Half the Human Experience*, D. C. Heath and Co., Lexington, U.S.A., 1976.
Home Office. *Equality for Women*, Cmnd., 5724, H.M.S.O., 1974.
A. Hunt. *A Survey of Women's Employment*, Volume 1, The Report, Government Social Survey, H.M.S.O., 1968.
The Law Commission. No. 86, Family Law – *Third report on Family Property: The Matrimonial Home (co-ownership and occupation rights) and Household Goods*, H.M.S.O., 1978.
M. Leevers. *Violence in Marriage*, S.H.A.C., 1976.
M. Leevers and P. Thynne. *A Woman's Place*, S.H.A.C., 1979.
E. E. Maccoby and C. N. Jacklin. *The Psychology of Sex Differences*, Oxford University Press, 1975.

Manchester Law Centre. Women's Handbook No. 2, *Getting Your Own Home,* Undated.

M.I.N.D. *Room to Let,* M.I.N.D., 1976.

E. Moberly Bell. *Octavia Hill,* Constable and Co., 1942.

N.A.B. *Homeless Single Persons,* H.M.S.O., 1966.

National Council for the Single Woman and her Dependants. *The Single Woman with Dependants,* N.C.S.W.D., 1969.

National Council for the Single Woman and her Dependants. *Single Women caring for their Dependants,* N.C.S.W.D., 1978.

National Women's Aid Federation. *Battered Women, Refuges and Women's Aid,* N.W.A.F., Undated.

O.P.C.S. *Hostels and Lodgings for Single People* by P. Wingfield Digby, H.M.S.O., 1976.

J. Pahl. *A Refuge for Battered Women,* D.H.S.S., H.M.S.O., 1978.

E. Pizzey. *Scream quietly or the neighbours will hear,* Penguin, 1974.

E. Sturges-Jones and S. Hewitt (editors). *Women in Politics,* Conservative Central Office, 1980.

M. E. H. Smith. *Guide to Housing,* Housing Centre Trust, 1977.

M. E. Tabor. *Octavia Hill,* The Sheldon Press, 1927.

J. Todd and L. Jones. *Matrimonial Property,* Social Survey Division, O.P.C.S., H.M.S.O., 1972.

A. Tinker. *Housing the Elderly near Relatives: Moving and Other Options,* D.O.E., Housing Development Directorate, Occasional Paper 1/80, H.M.S.O., 1980.

A. Tinker. *Housing the Elderly: How successful are Granny Annexes?,* D.O.E., Housing Development Directorate, Occasional Paper 1/76, H.M.S.O., Reprinted 1980.

J. Tunnard. *No Father, No Home?,* Poverty Pamphlet 28, C.P.A.G., 1976.

J. Tunnard. *Women and Housing – Owner Occupation,* C.P.A.G., 1978.

J. Tunnard and C. Whately. *Rights Guide for Home Owners,* C.P.A.G. and S.H.A.C., 1979.

E. Vallance. *Women in The House,* The Athlone Press, 1979.